WORLD HISTORY SERIES ■ ■ ■

The History of Rock and Roll

by
Adam Woog

Lucent Books, P.O. Box 289011, San Diego, CA 92198-9011

For Leah and Karen, who put up with
(and sometimes share) my musical tastes.

Library of Congress Cataloging-in-Publication Data

Woog, Adam, 1953–
    The history of rock and roll / by Adam Woog.
        p. cm.—(The world history series)
    Includes bibliographical references and index.
    Summary: Traces the history and evolution of rock music
from the early days of rock and roll through the present day.
    ISBN 1-56006-498-6   (lib. bdg. : alk. paper)
    1. Rock music—History and criticism—Juvenile literature.
[1. Rock Music.]   I. Title. II. Series.
ML3534.W64   1999
781.66'09—DC21   98–53048
                                                             CIP
                                                             MN

Contents

Foreword

Each year on the first day of school, nearly every history teacher faces the task of explaining why his or her students should study history. One logical answer to this question is that exploring what happened in our past explains how the things we often take for granted—our customs, ideas, and institutions—came to be. As statesman and historian Winston Churchill put it, "Every nation or group of nations has its own tale to tell. Knowledge of the trials and struggles is necessary to all who would comprehend the problems, perils, challenges, and opportunities which confront us today." Thus, a study of history puts modern ideas and institutions in perspective. For example, though the founders of the United States were talented and creative thinkers, they clearly did not invent the concept of democracy. Instead, they adapted some democratic ideas that had originated in ancient Greece and with which the Romans, the British, and others had experimented. An exploration of these cultures, then, reveals their very real connection to us through institutions that continue to shape our daily lives.

Another reason often given for studying history is the idea that lessons exist in the past from which contemporary societies can benefit and learn. This idea, although controversial, has always been an intriguing one for historians. Those who agree that society can benefit from the past often quote philosopher George Santayana's famous statement, "Those who cannot remember the past are condemned to repeat it." Historians who subscribe to Santayana's philosophy believe that, for example, studying the events that led up to the major world wars or other significant historical events would allow society to chart a different and more favorable course in the future.

Just as difficult as convincing students to realize the importance of studying history is the search for useful and interesting supplementary materials that present historical events in a context that can be easily understood. The volumes in Lucent Books' World History Series attempt to present a broad, balanced, and penetrating view of the march of history. Ancient Egypt's important wars and rulers, for example, are presented against the rich and colorful backdrop of Egyptian religious, social, and cultural developments. The series engages the reader by enhancing historical events with these cultural contexts. For example, in *Ancient Greece*, the text covers the role of women in that society. Slavery is discussed in *The Roman Empire*, as well as how slaves earned their freedom. The numerous and varied aspects of everyday life in these and other societies are explored in each volume of the series. Additionally, the series covers the major political, cultural, and philosophical ideas as the torch of civilization is passed from ancient Mesopotamia and Egypt, through Greece, Rome, Medieval Europe, and other world cultures, to the modern day.

The material in the series is formatted in a thorough, precise, and organized manner. Each volume offers the reader a comprehensive and clearly written overview of broad historical context. For example, *The Italian Renaissance* begins with a discussion of the High Middle Ages and the loss of central control that allowed certain Italian cities to develop artistically. The book ends by looking forward to the Reformation and interpreting the societal changes that grew out of the Renaissance. Thus, students are not only involved in an historical era, but also enveloped by the events leading up to that era and the events following it.

One important and unique feature in the World History Series is the primary and secondary source quotations that richly supplement each volume. These quotes are useful in a number of ways. First, they allow students access to sources they would not normally be exposed to because of the difficulty and obscurity of the original source. The quotations range from interesting anecdotes to farsighted cultural perspectives and are drawn from historical witnesses both past and present. Second, the quotes demonstrate how and where historians themselves derive their information on the past as they strive to reach a consensus on historical events. Lastly, all of the quotes are footnoted, familiarizing students with the citation process and allowing them to verify quotes and/or look up the original source if the quote piques their interest.

Finally, the books in the World History Series provide a detailed launching point for further research. Each book contains a bibliography specifically geared toward student research. A second, annotated bibliography introduces students to all the sources the author consulted when compiling the book. A chronology of important dates gives students an overview, at a glance, of the topic covered. Where applicable, a glossary of terms is included.

In short, the series is designed not only to acquaint readers with the basics of history, but also to make them aware that their lives are a part of an ongoing human saga. Perhaps they will then come to the same realization as famed historian Arnold Toynbee. In his monumental work, *A Study of History*, he wrote about becoming aware of history flowing through him in a mighty current, and of his own life "welling like a wave in the flow of this vast tide."

Important Dates in the History of Rock and Roll

1938
Eddie Durham of the Count Basie band makes what are probably the first recorded electric guitar solos.

1946
Rhythm-and-blues bandleader Joe Liggins's single "Sugar Lump" is called "right rhythmic rock and roll music" in a music-industry trade journal, the first known use of the phrase in print.

1951
Ike Turner, with vocalist Jackie Brenston, records "Rocket '88," widely regarded as the first genuine rock-and-roll song; the first rock radio show, Alan Freed's *Moondog's Rock 'n' Roll Party*, debuts on station WJW in Cleveland, Ohio.

1953
Bill Haley records "Crazy Man Crazy," the first rock-and-roll single to be a nation-wide hit and to make the *Billboard* charts.

1954
Elvis Presley records his first single, "That's All Right (Mama)"/"Blue Moon of Kentucky."

1955
"Maybellene" becomes the first of many hits by Chuck Berry; Fats Domino records his first national hit, "Ain't That a Shame"; "Tutti Frutti," the first hit record by Little Richard, is recorded.

1956
Elvis scores his first national hit, "Heartbreak Hotel."

1957
Top-forty radio formatting debuts on station KOWH in Omaha, Nebraska.

1958
Ray Charles, widely considered the father of soul music, has his first national hit with "I've Got a Woman."

1959
The payola scandal rocks the music industry.

1960
Motown, the most important black music production company of the 1960s, scores the first of its many hits.

1962
Philles Records, the independent label of legendary producer Phil Spector, is formed.

1964
The Beatles make their first appearances in America and touch off both Beatlemania and the British Invasion.

1965
Bob Dylan appears at the Newport Folk Festival with an electric band, infuriating folk purists but inaugurating the folk-rock era.

1966
Aretha Franklin, "Lady Soul," records the first of her classic hits.

1967
During the Summer of Love, the Beatles

release *Sgt. Pepper's Lonely Hearts Club Band,* the most emblematic album of the sixties; the Monterey International Pop Festival ushers in the age of rock festivals.

1969
The Woodstock and Altamont festivals represent the best and the worst of the rock-festival era.

1969–1970
The Beatles break up.

1970–1971
Three major figures in sixties rock—Janis Joplin, Jimi Hendrix, and Jim Morrison—die of drug- and alcohol-related causes.

1971
Carole King's *Tapestry* ushers in the singer-songwriter movement; the movie *The Harder They Come* introduces Jamaican reggae music to mainstream America.

1976
The punk revolution explodes virtually simultaneously in London and New York.

1977
Saturday Night Fever is released, the focal point of disco.

1979
The first mainstream rap single, "Rapper's Delight" by the Sugar Hill Gang, is released.

1980–1985
The audio cassette, compact disc, and personal cassette machines are introduced.

1981
MTV is introduced.

1982
Michael Jackson's *Thriller* and its accompanying videos set new records for sales and new standards for music videos.

1984
Bruce Springsteen, rock's most important traditionalist, releases his breakthrough album *Born in the USA*; Bob Geldof organizes the recording of "Do They Know It's Christmas?" as a benefit for Ethiopian famine relief, inaugurating an era of charity recordings and performances by rockers; the Rock and Roll Hall of Fame inducts its first members.

1992
Grunge, the dominant form of rock in the nineties, goes nationwide when Nirvana's "Smells Like Teen Spirit" becomes a surprise hit.

1994
Nirvana leader Kurt Cobain commits suicide.

1995
The Rock and Roll Hall of Fame and Museum opens in Cleveland, Ohio.

1996
A massive television documentary and CD retrospective of the Beatles make them more popular than ever.

The River of Rock

Rock won't eliminate your problems. But it will let you sort of dance all over them.

— Pete Townshend of the Who

It was the background music for the events of my life. My theme music.

— Jerry Garcia of the Grateful Dead

Once upon a time, when rock and roll was new, the music industry ignored it. Record company executives, radio station managers, and concert promoters on the whole thought it was a silly fad that would soon disappear.

They were wrong.

Rock and roll, which later became rock, is the dominant music of the twentieth century. Nearly a half century since the first rockers strutted on stage, the music is still very much here. Around the world rock is, as Jerry Garcia put it, not only the theme music for the lives of millions, capable of carrying tremendous weight and influence, but it is also the background music of daily life, commonplace on radio and television, in supermarkets and malls.

The River

Defining rock is notoriously hard. Ask a dozen musicians or fans to describe it, and the result will be a dozen answers—each different, all valid.

Sometimes rock is silly pop music, sometimes an emotional cry from the soul. Sometimes it's dance music with an irresistible beat. Sometimes it's disposable junk, sometimes high art capable of delivering power, beauty, and meaning.

Perhaps the best definition is the broadest. Journalist Bill Flanagan writes that rock's many branches stem from the first rock-and-roll singers of the 1950s to include "folk and funk and fusion and everything else east of Lionel Ritchie, west of Miles Davis, north of George Jones, and south of Pete Seeger."[1]

All these branches are part of a rich and varied tradition. Rock's ancestry winds through centuries of African and European music, and its immediate ancestors are idioms in American popular music that range from the blues to gospel, commercial pop to bluegrass. More recently, rock has also been deeply influenced by "outsider" styles from around the world.

This history—its evolution, its influences, its divergent paths—is intense and complicated. Dividing rock history into eras is convenient but misleading since styles have a habit of never quite going away. Yesterday's sensations may be forgotten today, only to be "rediscovered" tomorrow. Others develop and grow, never fully losing their audiences.

Rock history can thus be thought of as a river; it continually carries material from upstream, mixes the old stuff with new material, and sends it all downstream. Rock also has a way of rediscovering its deepest roots every few years. Critic and historian Robert Palmer notes that the music's history is "a matter of cycles within cycles . . . a developing idiom that periodically refreshes itself by drinking from its own deepest wellsprings."[2]

The Earthquakes

Despite this constant renewal, all popular music, rock included, periodically experiences the doldrums. This happens, in large part, as the music industry tries to make it as palatable as possible to the widest audience, watering it down to make it commercially successful. Fans will turn away, however, if the music becomes so blandly commercial that it loses its spice. This has happened several times to rock, each time prompting predictions that the music is dead, that it has run its course. But rock has always experienced a jolt— an earthquake of sorts—that has brought it back to life.

The first jolt, the one that first gave life to rock and roll, came in the 1950s, when a small group of wildly gifted, gleefully rebellious musicians began ripping up the stagnant pop music scene. They came from musically rich cities like New Orleans and Memphis, and they recorded their music on shoestrings in a succession of scrappy little studios.

Inevitably, the power and creativity of this first wave of rock began to grow dull. Further earthquakes, notably the British

Modern Folk Music

Rock and roll is notoriously hard to define, notes Paul Williams in The Map: Rediscovering Rock and Roll.

"Chuck Berry could tell you what rock and roll is, and so could Jimi Hendrix, or John Lennon, or Gordon Gano [of the band Violent Femmes]. But no two of them would tell you the same thing. I like this comment by Michael Steele of the Bangles, quoted in *People* magazine: 'We're just reinterpreting sounds. The Beatles interpreted Chuck Berry and Buddy Holly. It's a never-ending process. Basically it's all modern folk music, passed down through generations.' That's true."

*Seventy-thousand
screaming fans packed
Seattle's Kingdome for a
Rolling Stones concert in
1981. In the fifties and
sixties many believed rock
and roll was just a
passing fad that would
soon die. Through
constant reinvention and
innovation, rock and roll
continues to survive and
thrive.*

Invasion and psychedelia, were needed to stir things up. In the meantime, what had begun as music for dance and entertainment turned into a genuine art form; rock and roll became rock. Audiences also grew larger, as succeeding generations of fans came of age. By the seventies, rock was played in huge arenas, and a new class of entertainer—the millionaire rock star—had been born.

Then came another bracing jolt, as the punk revolution of 1976 forced rock back to its raw, rebellious roots. Punk stripped the music to its bare essentials. Furthermore, punk's democratic spirit and do-it-yourself attitude (Anybody can be in a band! Who cares if you can't play an instrument?) were direct confrontations to the mainstream music industry.

There have been further developments since 1976—post-punk, MTV, thrash metal, rap, grunge—and there will be more in the future. Before exploring these rich possibilities, however, it is important to look at the roots of rock and roll: the music that first gave it life.

1 Growing from the Roots

E pluribus unum: *"out of many, one."*
That's what it says on the dollar bill, and it's
as good a motto as you can find for the way
popular music developed in this country.

— writer Ed Ward

Americans invented the blues: This is what
we have got to be proud of. It ain't the nu-
clear stuff, it's not putting the man on the
moon, it's the blues.

— author Ken Kesey

In the early days of America, different strands of popular music arrived—as did Americans themselves—from many parts of the world. Black slaves brought African songs, Irish and English immigrants brought jigs and reels, and German and Polish settlers brought polkas. For all of these people, music served as a powerful reminder of a homeland far away.

Musical styles were generally divided by racial, social, and religious barriers. Religious people listened to religious music and condemned those who preferred "the devil's music." The upper classes preferred classical or light classical, and they disdained vulgar popular music. The racial barrier was probably the strongest, however: White audiences almost exclusively listened to music by white musicians in familiar European styles; black people, likewise, listened almost exclusively to black musicians playing in styles familiar to them.

Another barrier to the intermingling of styles was simply geographical. Pockets of distinctive regional music developed in culturally rich cities such as Nashville, Chicago, New York, Kansas City, New Orleans, and Memphis. Travel was difficult, however, and often musicians were not heard outside their immediate regions.

Beginning early in the century, radio and phonographs began breaking down these barriers. Thanks to these technological innovations, a fiddler from Kentucky could hear a guitarist from Chicago; New Yorkers could hear the driving rhythms of Kansas City bands, and the Kansas City musicians could hear the sophisticated sounds of New York jazz bands.

Gradually, too, strictly divided styles began to blend and borrow from one another. One result of this blending of idioms, especially black and white styles, was a new music called rock and roll.

It was a slow process that took place over many years and in many places. In recorded music, black and white music had already begun mixing it up by the 1930s, as when, for example, black jazz trumpeter Louis Armstrong recorded with white bluegrass singer Jimmie Rodgers. The process had probably started informally long before then, though. As Bill Flanagan writes,

> The two traditions crossed over and influenced one another all the time, though they were formally as separate as the front gate and the back door. One reason black and white [musicians] didn't always acknowledge how much they lifted from each other is that black and white men often resist admitting how much they have in common.[3]

Artists like jazz trumpeter Louis Armstrong helped break down racial barriers that kept certain styles of music and musicians from intermingling.

Out of Africa

Perhaps the most important elements in rock's ancestry came from Africa, brought to the American South by slaves and developed further by their descendants. White traditions have been vital in rock's development, but most historians and fans agree that the primary influence has been black. Peter Gabriel, an English rocker who has been deeply influenced by music from around the world, states, "Part of what we consider our fundamental rock and roll heritage originated in Africa. Period."[4]

Perhaps the most important of these influences is an emphasis on a steady beat —a *rocking* beat—adopted from the complex drumming styles that are common across Africa. Because drums were often forbidden to slaves on the theory that powerful instruments could incite them to rebellion, slaves often created their rhythmic songs using only hand claps, foot stomps, and voices.

Vocal styles borrowed from Africa were also important predecessors to rock. One example was the technique called call and response, in which a chorus echoed a lead singer. Typically, the lead singer also used a high degree of improvisation and an emotion-filled tone that seemed rough and coarse by European standards. Furthermore, musicians, singers, and audience members alike often entered a kind of ecstatic trance state that was called "getting happy." This became a cornerstone of both the black church tradition and, later, rock and roll.

Some of the earliest recorded examples of black music were made by a father-and-son team of musicologists, John and

African vocal and percussion styles, brought to America by slaves, heavily influenced the blues. The blues, in turn, influenced many of the first major rock stars.

Alan Lomax. In the 1930s the Lomaxes recorded a significant collection of American folk music for the Library of Congress. This series includes "field shouts," songs used to maintain steady rhythms while picking cotton or otherwise working in fields, and songs sung by prison chain gangs.

One example, a 1934 recording of a church congregation singing a type of song called a ring shout, has words that seem like direct ancestors of rock and roll:

> O my Lord
> Well well well
> I've gotta rock . . .[5]

The Blues

Perhaps the most important style of music that developed from African influences was the blues. It is not an exaggeration to say that the blues is the basic vocabulary of rock.

The blues emerged in the early part of the century in the fertile Mississippi delta as a style of acoustic (or "country") singing and playing that used commonly available instruments such as guitars, pianos, harmonicas, basses made from washtubs, and bones or washboards for percussion. The National steel-body guitar, often used with a slide to produce its characteristic haunting sound, was favored in those preamplification days for its loud, bright tone.

The blues sound is created with "blue" or "bent" notes, formally the flattened third and seventh notes of a scale, which have a highly expressive and melancholy feel. Also typical of the blues are a simple structure, usually twelve bars with a repeated three-chord progression, and lyrics that express a bittersweet mixture of joy and pain.

The acknowledged king of early blues was Mississippian Robert Johnson, whose

Listening to the Source

In these passages, Eric Clapton, one of rock's most acclaimed guitarists, acknowledges the debt he owes to American bluesmen. The first quote is from Ward, Stokes, and Tucker's Rock of Ages, *the second is from* The Rolling Stone History of Rock and Roll.

"At first I played exactly like Chuck Berry for six or seven months. You couldn't have told the difference when I was with the Yardbirds. Then I got into older bluesmen. Because he was so readily available, I dug Big Bill Broonzy; then I heard a lot of cats I had never heard before: Robert Johnson and Skip James and Blind Boy Fuller. I just finally got completely overwhelmed in this brand-new world. I studied it and listened to it and went right down in it and came back up in it."

Legendary rock guitarist Eric Clapton developed his style by imitating blues guitarists.

"I copied most of my runs from B. B. [King] or Albert King or Freddie King. There's no reason why [other guitarists] should listen to me when they can listen to the masters, you know, the source."

rough, hard-drinking life set the standard for the classic bluesman. Johnson gained his mastery of the slide guitar, according to legend, after making a pact with the devil at "the crossroads" in Clarksdale, Mississippi; he produced only a handful of recordings before his death at age twenty —he was apparently poisoned by a jealous girlfriend.

During and after World War II, large numbers of African Americans moved from rural regions to cities in search of better jobs. Blues musicians were exposed to jazz and other sophisticated, big-city styles of popular music. At the same time, electrified instruments were more widely available.

Out of this combination of events emerged a type of amplified blues, harder edged and more aggressive. Memphis became a particular hotbed of this new urban style, nurturing such performers as singer-guitarist B. B. King and singer Bobby Bland. Chicago was the home of an important blues sound that was developed by artists such as singer-guitarist Muddy Waters and pianist Otis Spann.

The T-Bone Shuffle

In Los Angeles, meanwhile, Texas-born guitarist T-Bone Walker was experimenting with a still-developing, thrilling new invention: the electric guitar. In time the electric guitar would be a fundamental part of rock and roll; in Walker's day, however, it was merely a clumsy, erratic, intriguing novelty.

Two other guitar pioneers made music that crossed the boundary between the blues and another evolving music: jazz. Charlie Christian, who played with Benny Goodman's swing band, and Eddie Durham, with Count Basie's Kansas City orchestra, also used electric guitars early on. The records Durham made in 1938 with Basie, in fact, were probably the first electric guitar solos on record.

Basie and his band were the premier exponents of a brand of jazz called jump blues. This lively dance music was fast spreading from its Midwest origins to replace established jazz idioms, which had developed in New Orleans and Chicago. Jump blues was driven by a rocking rhythm section, tough tenor saxophone soloists, and a powerhouse horn section that specialized in repetitive phrases called riffs. As the name implies, it was also heavily influenced by the blues.

Despite the importance of Durham and Christian, however, Walker was the most influential guitarist of his day. He was the first, for instance, to fully explore now-common techniques like dynamic changes, string bending, vibrato, long single-note runs, and a boogie beat he called the Texas or T-bone shuffle.

Walker's style was a huge influence on other guitarists of the day, and he continues to be an inspiration. A guitarist today may not even have heard of T-Bone Walker, but his or her style will undoubtedly reflect Walker's pioneering work. As rock critic Robert Palmer notes, "This is what we mean when we call rock and roll a *living* tradition."[6]

High Lonesome

As black music was evolving into styles like electric blues and jump blues, white musicians were creating other idioms. Dominating white pop music of the time were

Texas-born guitarist T-Bone Walker was one of the first musicians to experiment with electric guitars. His playing style was a tremendous influence on other guitarists of the day.

crooners like Frank Sinatra, who interpreted songs by composers like George Gershwin, and swing musicians, who played a sophisticated, "sweetened" version of black jazz.

More important to the history of rock and roll, however, was the development of country music and its close relative, bluegrass. Both drew heavily on traditional Irish-English music, typified by storytelling songs; stringed instruments such as the banjo, mandolin, and fiddle; and vocals characterized by "high lonesome" close harmonies.

Bluegrass was often the focus of dances in isolated mountain or prairie communities. Country music, the more commercial branch, was centered in the recording base of Nashville, Tennessee. It gave the music's traditional elements a glossy pop overlay with modern instruments, especially the trademark twang of the pedal steel guitar.

A related hybrid was Western swing, which combined elements of country with the powerful rhythms of horn-driven swing jazz and many other eccentric elements, even the polkas of German and Polish immigrant groups. Western swing's best-known proponent was Bob Wills and his Texas Playboys, whose many hits included the now-classic "San Antonio Rose."

Among the most influential early country/bluegrass artists were Jimmie Rodgers from Mississippi and a pair of siblings from Alabama, the Delmore Brothers. The most important of all, however, was Hank Williams, the father of modern country music. (His son, Hank Williams Jr., is also a noted singer.)

Growing up in Alabama, Williams played with blues artists and learned guitar from a black street musician. He later mixed black and white styles to create an extremely popular style that he dubbed honky-tonk. The singer's magnetic stage presence, aching voice, and beautifully crafted songs set a high standard for future country music. They appealed to black audiences as well; many black musicians, including Ray Charles, have noted their affection for Williams's music.

Not Ashamed

Sam Phillips had a long history of recording blues and country groups. In Robert Palmer's Rock and Roll: An Unruly History *he comments on his recording style.*

"I didn't want to get these people in some . . . studio and lead them astray from what they had been used to doing. To put it another way, I didn't try to take them uptown and dress them up. If they had broken-down equipment or their instruments were ragged, I didn't want them to feel ashamed. I wanted them to go ahead and play the way they were used to playing. Because the expression was the thing."

Among the best of Williams's self-written songs are "Jambalaya," "I'm So Lonesome I Could Cry," and "Your Cheatin' Heart." Though they may seem clichéd today, these intense, plain-spoken songs of lost love and hard drinking were bold departures from the bland pop familiar to most white audiences of the day. Paul Friedlander writes that Williams "provided an alternative to the 'June, croon, spoon' worldview of contemporary popular music."[7]

"Good Rockin' Tonight"

A final element in the genesis of rock and roll was a hybrid music called rhythm and blues, or R&B. R&B drew its main inspiration from a merger of jump blues and pop vocals, blending the characteristic emphasis on the backbeat and "gutty" tenor sax solos of jump blues with showy, gospel-influenced vocals.

The term *rhythm and blues* was coined sometime in the 1940s—the exact date is uncertain—by Jerry Wexler, a writer for the music-industry magazine *Billboard*. (Wexler later became a cofounder of Atlantic, one of the most important blues/R&B record labels.) The phrase was eventually used as a catchall for all black pop music, replacing the archaic term *race music*.

A number of singers made R&B recordings in the late 1940s that skirt close

Hank Williams was one of the first musicians to blend white and black styles of music. He called this style honky-tonk, and it set the standard for much of today's popular country music.

to what can be considered rock and roll. These include Roy Brown's "Good Rockin' Tonight," Amos Milburn's "Chicken Shack Boogie," and Little Willie Littlefield's "K. C. Loving," later rewritten into a rock standard called "Kansas City."

For all intents and purposes, the pieces of rock and roll were ready. All the music needed now was a group of artists willing to bring the ingredients together—and to find an audience.

Chapter

2 The First Rock Explosion

Before Elvis, there was nothing.

— John Lennon

The exact point at which rock and roll coalesced is shrouded in mystery, and there are many worthy contenders for the title of first rock-and-roll record.

Some music scholars say that it was Roy Brown's 1948 R&B hit "Good Rockin' Tonight." (The same song was later an even bigger hit for Elvis Presley.) Others point to "Rock All Night Long" by a New York vocal group, the Ravens, released the same year. Still others champion a 1949 single, "Rock Awhile," by an obscure Houston guitarist, Goree Carter.

Each of these records had the necessary basic ingredients, and all are impressive candidates. Perhaps the strongest contender, however, is "Rocket '88," recorded in Memphis in March 1951. With its grainy vocal, fuzzy guitar sound, wild sax solo, and subject matter (the singer's car), it is a superb prediction of the direction of early rock and roll.

The leader of the band behind "Rocket '88" was Ike Turner. Years before he formed his famous soul revue with then-wife Tina, Ike was a popular bandleader in the Memphis area. On "Rocket '88," how-

ever, saxophonist Jackie Brenston was the singer, and the record is credited to him.

The story behind the song's distinctive guitar sound illustrates the casual nature of pop record production in the 1950s. Lead guitarist Willie Kizart's amp had fallen from his car on the way to the studio, and the speaker cone burst. Producer Sam Phillips, later a legendary figure through his work with Elvis Presley, recalls, "It would probably have taken a couple of days [to fix it], so we started playing around with the damn thing. I stuffed a little paper in there where the speaker cone was ruptured, and it sounded good."[8]

The Independents

"Rocket '88" and other "protorock" records, for all their charms, were strictly localized phenomena. Ike Turner was a star around Memphis, but neither he nor any other early rock artist was yet able to score a national hit.

One reason for this was that their recordings were made by small companies with shoestring budgets and limited distribution. None of the big record companies thought that R&B was worth pushing since the vast majority of the pop audience was

The First Rock and Roll?

Robert Palmer's Rock and Roll: An Unruly History *contains this comment from bandleader and musician Ike Turner on the genesis of the first rock and roll.*

"I don't think that when somebody puts a name on something, that makes it the beginning of it. [Jazzmen] Fats Waller, Cab Calloway— if you just take the color off of it, man, these guys rocked and rolled way back then. So how could the first rock and roll be when they decided to name it rock and roll? Now, I can sit right here at this piano and play you jazz, I can play you country, I can play you anything you name, and to me it's all the same. How can you say what I play is r&b? If you want to classify it as far as the music is concerned, that's okay. But if you're going to classify it because of my color, well, then I don't know about that."

Ike Turner, one of America's first rock and rollers.

white—at least that part of the pop audience with money to spend. The big record companies concentrated instead on mainstream pop.

This left R&B open to the small, independent labels. In Los Angeles the Aladdin and Specialty labels recorded R&B singers like Amos Milburn and Larry Williams. In Memphis, Sam Phillips nurtured his Sun imprint. Labels like Ace were documenting the lively New Orleans sound.

The Chess brothers, based in Chicago, were typical. They visited the Deep South twice a year to record musicians for their small, blues-based Chess label. They carried with them a cumbersome tape recorder powered by a portable gas generator, so that they could record anywhere. More than once they lugged their equipment into the middle of a cotton field to record a musician on his lunch break.

These little labels, however, lacked the resources to take their music across the country. Rock and roll existed, and it was ready for America to discover it, but a national hit was needed first.

"Rock Around the Clock"

That honor went to 1953's "Crazy Man Crazy," the first certified rock and roll record to make the *Billboard* pop charts.

The singer was a former country musician named Bill Haley. The fact that he was a white man playing in a black style doubtless helped Haley's breakthrough success. Dave Bartholomew, a New Orleans producer, says, "We had rhythm and blues for

Bill Haley put rock and roll on the musical map in 1953 when his song "Crazy Man Crazy" became a national hit. Haley later went to the top of the Billboard charts with "Rock Around the Clock."

many, many a year, and here come in a couple of white people and they call it rock and roll, and it was rhythm and blues all the time!"[9]

Haley followed his hit with others, including a tame version of "Shake, Rattle, and Roll," a song first popularized by blues shouter Big Joe Turner. Haley's "Rock Around the Clock" became a number-one hit after it was featured in *The Blackboard Jungle*, a popular movie about teenage rebellion.

Haley's career was short, however. Uncharismatic, pudgy, slightly balding, and self-conscious about a blind eye, he never had the chance to capitalize on his stardom. His wooden singing and competent but dull band, meanwhile, paled in comparison with the unbridled energy of later musicians.

Many fans and scholars have downplayed Haley's role in rock history. Nonetheless, his tentative blend of white and black styles made him an important rock-and-roll pioneer. In an interview in the 1970s, Haley wistfully commented on his lack of recognition: "The story has got pretty crowded as to who was the Father of Rock and Roll. I haven't done much in life except that. And I'd like to get credit for it."[10]

The First True Rock and Roller?

Even as Haley was beginning to fade from the public eye, big things were stirring elsewhere. Between 1953 and 1955, the first true rockers—a tidal wave that included Chuck Berry, Fats Domino, and Little Richard—swept across America.

The honor paid to Chuck Berry as the first inductee to the Rock and Roll Hall of Fame is an indication of his importance to the music. Many consider Berry the first true rock and roller because of both his music and his bad-boy personal life; he has been the center of controversy for decades, including two stints in prison.

Berry's formative years demonstrated the powerful effect of intermingled regional styles. Growing up in St. Louis, Missouri, he absorbed everything from Chicago blues and Midwest jump bands to southern country.

He later worked as a beautician while leading a blues band and writing songs he hoped would appeal to teenagers. His break came when Chess Records bought his "Ida Red"; the Chess executives didn't like the title, however, and convinced Berry to change it to "Maybellene." The song, released in 1955, reached the top ten and was the first of Berry's many hits.

The best of Berry's songs are models of economy and wit, full of clever wordplay and simple but potent images. "Maybellene," "School Day," "Sweet Little Sixteen," "Johnny B. Goode," "The Promised Land," and "Roll Over Beethoven"—to name only a handful—went on to become a part of America's pop heritage. Rock critic and journalist Ben Fong-Torres writes that they are "a body of highly American imagery from which rock & roll continues to feed."[11]

Berry's patented guitar licks and manic "duckwalk" set a performance standard for years to come. Like T-Bone Walker before him, Berry was an innovator whose influence is still felt. Rock critic and journalist Robert Christgau wryly notes, "He taught George Harrison [of the Beatles] and Keith Richards [of the Rolling Stones] to play guitar long before he met either."[12]

Chuck Berry is considered by many to be the first true rock star. His influence on rock music was so great that he was awarded the first induction into the Rock and Roll Hall of Fame.

"The Fat Man"

New Orleans has been the cradle of many memorable musical styles, including a vibrant R&B scene. In the early 1950s, that scene produced a musician who perfectly summed up the city's rich mixture of black, white, French, Spanish, and Creole cultures—and who also rocked.

Antoine "Fats" Domino began building a strong local reputation with his first single, "The Fat Man," in 1949, when he was twenty-one. By the time rock and roll began to be felt nationwide, therefore, he was a seasoned musician, and his records were routinely selling over a half-million copies apiece.

Antoine "Fats" Domino was a rock pioneer who had tremendous pop success. With the exception of Elvis Presley, Fats Domino sold more records than any other fifties rocker.

Domino did not have a national hit, however, until "Ain't That a Shame" in 1955. The tunes that followed—"Blue Monday," "Blueberry Hill," "I'm Walkin'"—proved he could sustain his hitmaking on a national level. Including his last million-seller, "Walkin' to New Orleans" in 1960, Domino racked up twenty-three gold singles (singles that sold a million or more). In all, he sold over 65 million records, more than any 1950s rock pioneer except Elvis Presley.

Domino's charm came from several sources. His genial, sweetly rotund persona was never threatening, unlike other

rockers. Musically, his records were an appealing blend of his unique half-blues and half-country piano style, loose but rocking arrangements, and distinctive, lazy Creole accent. The combination made perfect pop records, both as individual as a thumbprint and as familiar as an old shoe. New Orleans studio owner and engineer Cosimo Matassa comments, "Domino, he was creative. No matter what he does comes through. He could be singing the national anthem, you'd still know by the time he said two words it was him, obviously, unmistakably, and pleasurably him."[13]

The Georgia Peach

Little Richard (nicknamed "the Georgia Peach" for his Georgia roots) may not have been the most gifted of the early rockers, but he was the wildest. Richard ironically called himself "the Bronze Liberace." The title reflected how his gleefully over-the-top style (towering hair, heavy makeup, flamboyant wardrobe, and teasing sexuality) echoed that of Liberace, a pop pianist who had delighted and scandalized a previous generation. No one had more attitude than Little Richard.

Richard Penniman was born in Macon, Georgia, into a religious family. They listened to mainstream pop, but Richard had to sneak around to play "the devil's music"—the raunchy material that he secretly loved. He recalls, "Bing Crosby, 'Pennies from Heaven,' Ella Fitzgerald, was all I heard. And I knew there was something that could be louder than that, but I didn't know where to find it. And I found it was me."[14]

Richard toured with medicine shows and R&B bands before developing his own flashy style and forming a band. His first big hit, "Tutti Frutti," sold a respectable half-million singles in 1955.

"Tutti Frutti" and successors like "Long Tall Sally" and "Good Golly Miss Molly," with their nonsense lyrics and rough energy, made the Georgia Peach a star, especially among fans who delighted in scandalizing their parents. Little Richard also became famous for his excessive on-tour partying; as he recalls, "The river was running. The river of loot. And I was on the bank."[15]

But Little Richard was always torn between two extremes: the extravagant rock-and-roll lifestyle and a deeply devout religious faith. In the years since he exploded on the scene, the Georgia Peach has periodically abandoned music in favor of Bible study, popping up now and again to loudly proclaim, to anyone who will listen, that he is the true father of rock and roll.

A King Is Born

Chuck Berry, Fats Domino, and Little Richard were only the tip of the iceberg. Between 1955 and 1958, they were joined by dozens of other rockers. The roll call is long and distinguished, but one man, more than any other, defined this golden age of classic rock and roll.

Perhaps no other performer has had a greater impact on pop culture than Elvis Presley. More than twenty years after his death, his name, his face, and his music still evoke instant recognition even in distant corners of the world. For many people Elvis was—and is—rock and roll. In a saying frequently attributed to Bruce Springsteen, "There have been contenders, but there is only one King."

Elvis did not invent rock and roll. He was not the first to bring black and white musical styles together. It can be argued that he was not the music's most gifted

With his heavy makeup and outrageous hair, Little Richard introduced a flamboyant, over-the-top style to the rock scene of the 1950s. He is one of the many who stake a claim to being the true father of rock and roll.

But the Kids Like It

"In one review Jack Gould, the television critic for the New York *Times*, wrote 'Mr. Presley has no discernable singing ability. His specialty is rhythm, songs which he renders in an undistinguished whine; his phrasing, if it can be called that, consists of the stereotyped variations that go with a beginner's aria in a bathtub. . . . His one specialty is an accented movement of the body that heretofore has been primarily identified with the repertoire of the blonde bombshells of the burlesque runway. The gyration never had anything to do with the world of popular music and still doesn't.' Jack O'Brien of the New York *Journal-American* agreed that 'Elvis Presley wiggled and wiggled with such abdominal gyrations that burlesque bombshell Georgia Southern really deserves equal time to reply in gyrating kind. He can't sing a lick, makes up for vocal shortcomings with the weirdest and plainly planned, suggestive animation short of an aborigine's mating dance.'"

singer. Nor did he write his own songs, relying instead on other (often mediocre) writers. Nonetheless, Elvis remains the single most important person in the development of rock and roll.

This is because he was gifted not only as a performer and a synthesizer of styles but also as a popularizer. He was the first person to bring rock and roll to a truly widespread, mixed-race audience by successfully merging the intensity of black music with a mournful hillbilly sound. In so doing, he introduced rock and roll to the world.

As a teenager fresh out of high school and working as a truck driver in Memphis, Presley made his first recording at a local studio. According to legend, it was a gift for his mother.

His voice caught the attention of the studio's owner. Sam Phillips, the producer of Ike Turner's "Rocket '88" and a fanatical champion of black music, had often remarked that he could make a fortune if he found a singer with the passion of a black artist and a face that would appeal to white audiences. He thought that Elvis might just be that singer.

Phillips teamed the young singer with two professional musicians, guitarist Scotty Moore and bassist Bill Black. After months of practice they released their first single in 1954. Its two songs reflected Presley's ability to span white and black styles. One side was a blues song, "That's All Right (Mama)," and the other was a sped-up version of a country waltz, "Blue Moon of Kentucky."

The record was a regional hit, and Presley's fame slowly grew. Under the direction of a wily manager, Colonel Tom Parker, the singer's career took off. After his Sun contract was sold to a major record company, RCA, for the unheard-of sum of thirty-five thousand dollars, Presley's "Heartbreak Hotel" was his first national hit in 1956—and the first volley in Parker's scheme to make "his boy" into the most successful entertainment figure of all time.

Rockabilly Lives

When Elvis left Sam Phillips's care, the producer's other protégés carried on the style he and Elvis had more or less invented: rockabilly.

The 1950s saw the beginning of the career of Elvis Presley, who many came to consider the king of rock and roll. In 1954 he released his first single, "That's All Right Mama."

In the late 1950s many southern musicians experimented with their own blends of country and rock. Standouts included the exquisite harmonies of the Everly Brothers, the heartbreakingly pure voice of Roy Orbison, and the playful, hiccuping vocals of Buddy Holly. Rockabilly, however, was the most radical of these fusions.

It had an unmistakable sound: up-tempo, with accented offbeats from a slapping bass, vocals with plenty of echo (the singers often sounded like they were in a sewer pipe), and snappy lyrics: "My gal is red hot! Your gal ain't doodly squat!" Looks were also important; musicians and fans alike dressed in elaborate "cat clothes" and slicked their hair into greasy pompadours.

There were many hopefuls, including Charlie Feathers, Gene Vincent, and Billy Lee Riley, but Carl Perkins, a gifted singer-writer-guitarist, was the heir apparent to rockabilly stardom. Though Elvis later made the song famous, Perkins's version of "Blue Suede Shoes" (which he wrote) was the first record to top the R&B, country, and pop charts simultaneously. Unfortunately, Perkins suffered a serious car accident just as the record was peaking, and his career never reached the heights once promised.

The wild rockabilly persona, meanwhile, was best illustrated by one performer. Jerry Lee Lewis, out of Ferriday, Louisiana, wasn't called "the Killer" for nothing.

In an era already dominated by the guitar, Lewis played an unlikely instrument: the piano. But he played it in an unforgettable way—with his feet and his fists, kicking over the stool, jumping on the piano, all the while growling and crooning into the microphone.

Lewis's handful of singles for Sun, including "Whole Lotta Shakin' Goin' On"

and "Great Balls of Fire," remain definitive recordings of the era.

Offstage he was equally famous for his nonstop drinking, womanizing, gun-toting, and overall rowdy behavior. Many critics feel he was as talented as his great rival Elvis, and that he might have become as big a commercial success were it not for his relentlessly threatening personal style.

Moondog Spreads the Word

In the early 1950s television was still a novelty. Radio was the main outlet for rockabilly and other kinds of new music exploding out of Los Angeles, Nashville, Memphis, Chicago, and New Orleans.

At the time few national radio networks existed. Instead, individual stations maintained loyal regional followings. Disc jockeys decided what songs to play and how often to play them. But stations and their audiences were also fairly strictly divided along racial lines at that point, and no white-oriented station touched rock and roll until Alan Freed came along.

Freed was hosting a classical show on WJW in Cleveland, Ohio, when he noticed in a record store that white teens were snapping up the latest rock-and-roll records. Freed talked his station manager into letting him host a show that spotlighted the music, and *Moondog's Rock 'n' Roll Party* debuted in June 1951.

The term *rock and roll* had been used in the black community for years, as both slang for sex and as a musical term. In 1946 *Billboard* had described R&B bandleader Joe Liggins's single "Sugar Lump" as "right rhythmic rock and roll music." On Freed's show, however, the phrase was

The Killer Cannot Be Upstaged

Jerry Lee Lewis was legendary for the fiery nature of both his temper and his stage act. In The Rolling Stone History of Rock and Roll, *John Grissim tells what happened when Lewis was denied the final spot on a concert bill that paired him with rival Chuck Berry.*

"Both Berry and Lewis had million-seller hits on the charts at the time and one night [emcee Alan] Freed flat-out insisted that Jerry Lee perform first. After a furious argument, Lewis obeyed. The story has it that he blew nonstop rock for a brutal 30 minutes and, during the final 'Whole Lot of Shakin',' poured lighter fluid over the piano and threw a match to it. As he stomped off the stage he hollered to the stage crew: 'I'd like to see any son of a bitch follow that!'"

Jerry Lee Lewis was known as "the Killer" because of his aggressive playing style as well as his reckless antics off the stage.

introduced to a mainstream audience for probably the first time.

Freed cultivated a crazed manner to go with the music: howling at the moon, beating his fist in time to the music in front of an open mike, talking in nonstop jive patter, and drinking openly while on the air. His show was an immediate hit with its target audience of "moondog daddies and crazy kittens," and Freed was soon imitated by others, including Dewey Phillips in Memphis, Poppa Stoppa in New Orleans, and the

Moondog Matinee

Ed Ward, in Rock of Ages, *sets the scene for a typical broadcast by legendary disc jockey Alan Freed.*

"On the air, the cultured Freed went wild. Todd Rhodes's 'Blues for Moondog,' a wailing sax solo, would start things off, with Freed, his mike open, howling like a demented coyote, and then he'd slide into the program with his patented gravelly voice, introducing the first record and getting ready to read a commercial. He kept a thick Cleveland phone book within easy reach, not far from his ever-present bottle, and over a particularly wild saxophone instrumental, he'd begin beating the rhythm out on the phone book, wailing 'Go! Go! Gogogogogogogo! Go! Go!' and screaming. It was crazy, it was close to anarchy. It was just what a very large number of teenagers had been waiting all their lives to hear."

Alan Freed was the first disc jockey to bring rock and roll to a mainstream radio audience.

gravel-voiced Bob "Wolfman Jack" Smith, whose high-powered "pirate" station in Mexico could be heard as far away as Canada.

Playing black music for white audiences, in those times of strong racial segregation, was a bold move. Freed did it because he wanted a hit show, but he also genuinely liked the music. "Cousin" Brucie Morrow, another DJ of the era, remarks, "Alan Freed became one of the bravest men ever to be a part of the record industry. . . . It was a kind of integrity that led him to play the R&B music that no one else would touch."[16]

"Whaddya Got?"

Radio could get the message out, but rock and roll would not have flourished without the explosive development of teen culture in America after the war, and its acceptance of the music.

Thanks to a strong postwar economy, American teens had far fewer responsibilities and far more leisure time and money than ever before. Translated into purchasing power, for the first time in history teens formed a pool of consumers controlling billions of disposable dollars.

Naturally, before long products specifically for teens appeared in quantity. As rock historian Paul Friedlander writes, "American business, recognizing the existence of a new consumer group, rushed to fill the void, providing 'essential' items such as clothes, cosmetics, fast food, cars —and music."[17]

Records (mostly singles with some long-play albums), radios (bulky table models or the thrilling new transistors), and hi-fi sets (stereo was still in the future) all absorbed the entertainment dollars teens were spending. However, the music industry often found it difficult to produce music that satisfied teens.

The pop music turned out by the major record labels was, almost without exception, bland and predictable. Teenagers preferred what they heard on small, scruffy, independent labels—the far more exciting and dangerous sounds of R&B and rock and roll.

The new music struck a chord of rebellion against the conformist, complacent society of the postwar years, an attitude summed up by Marlon Brando's famous line in *The Wild One*. In that movie a waitress asks Brando, who plays the leader of a mo-torcycle gang, what he's rebelling against. Brando coolly replies, "Whaddya got?"

An Evil Influence

Naturally, adults were disconcerted by such attitudes. How could kids be so rebellious when they had everything they wanted? Thus was laid one of the fundamental cornerstones of rock and roll: its long tradition of driving the old folks up the wall.

Parents and authorities, especially conservative lawmakers and clergy, increasingly railed against the influence of rock and roll on impressionable youth. Juvenile delinquents, race mixing, violence, vandalism— it was all clearly tied in with the music. Typical was a 1956 comment by the Reverend Albert Carter, a Pentecostal minister:

> The effect of rock and roll in young people is to turn them into devil worshippers; to stimulate self-expression through sex; to provoke lawlessness, impair nervous stability and destroy the sanctity of marriage. It is an evil influence on the youth of our country.[18]

The established music-industry response was to make rock tamer, more acceptable to a mainstream audience. It was the first attempt—but by no means the last—to tamp down rock and roll's unruly energy.

3 Pop Moves In: The Music Industry Discovers Rock and Roll

It's too late to quit—pass the dynamite, 'cause the fuse is lit.

— Leiber and Stoller, "Riot in Cell Block #9," recorded by the Coasters

Anyone who says rock & roll is a passing fad or a flash-in-the-pan trend along the music road has rocks in the head, dad!

— Alan Freed

Until the breakthrough success of Elvis, rock and roll was known to a relatively small group of fans. It was thus outside the notice of the established music industry; the amount of money rockers generated was tiny compared to mainstream pop artists of the day like Perry Como, Frank Sinatra, and Patti Page.

However, as rock and roll began to gain nationwide popularity (and make serious money), the record industry took notice. Between 1958 and 1963 the music industry moved to embrace the new music and rock and roll became big business.

By 1963 record companies were selling $100 million in singles, making another $1.3 billion in television profits, and still another half-billion from five hundred thousand jukeboxes spread across the country—and this was in America alone. An early 1960s press release from Decca Records boasted, "The recording industry, a fledgling during the heyday of vaudeville, has shown a steady, remarkable growth until today it stands as a major factor in the world's economy."[19]

The tendency in all musical styles, as they move from fringe phenomenon to mainstream entertainment, is to become watered down. This decrease in intensity makes the "product," as the music industry calls its creations, acceptable to the widest audience possible. Rock and roll was no exception. John Tobler, a veteran music writer, writes that beginning in 1958 there was "a distinct trend towards the widespread softening and dilution of rock 'n' roll into a more universally palatable product."[20]

In some ways this thinning-down led to inferior music. In other ways, however, the music benefited from more diversity and polish, from access to better production values, and from a new emphasis on more sophisticated songwriting. The rawness of rock and roll was meeting the polish of pop, and the result was not always bad.

Several new styles emerged and flourished in this atmosphere, from emotionally lush girl groups to silly dance crazes, from elaborate mini-symphonies to wildman instrumentals. Before, there had been essentially only one type of pop music in the mainstream; now there was something for everybody. Rock historian Ed Ward writes:

By 1963, there were surfers, folkies, teen idols, weird groups . . . that played guitar instrumentals and revived old records like "Louie Louie," twist maniacs, Brill Building popsters, girl groups, [and] Motown. . . . Now, everybody was forced to choose a side.[21]

A Shortage

One reason for such diversity was that the first wave of rockers fell by the wayside, at least temporarily. By the early 1960s, for a variety of reasons, rock and roll had a distinct shortage of stars.

It began in 1958, when Elvis's induction into the army put his meteoric rise on hold. Buddy Holly died in an airplane crash in 1959. Two promising rockabilly cats suffered a tragic car accident in 1960; Eddie Cochran died, and Gene Vincent, though not severely injured, never regained his momentum. Meanwhile, the Everly Brothers' career became a downward spiral of personal problems, including drug abuse, from which they never fully recovered.

Little Richard was caught between the pleasures of success and his long-held religious fervor. For the first of several times he abandoned entertainment in favor of the ministry. He says a powerful vision of doom persuaded him to quit rocking: "I got up from the piano and said, 'This is it. I am through. I am leaving show business to go back to God.'"[22]

Chuck Berry then disappeared into jail (he had hired a young woman to check hats in his St. Louis nightclub, and she turned out to be an underage prostitute). Finally, Jerry Lee Lewis also vanished in the wake of a scandal (he married his thirteen-year-old cousin); the Killer was forced to spend years in limbo before concert promoters and record companies would touch him.

The music industry rushed to fill the void at the top left by the absence of these stars, especially Elvis. Loved or hated, the charismatic Elvis could not be ignored, and a frantic search was on for a replacement. As rock historian Charlie Gillett writes, "Presley's dark, heavy features, greasy black hair, and surly expression became elements of an image that producers everywhere sought or attempted to re-create."[23]

Teen Idols

Chief among these suitors for the public's affections were the so-called teen idols. These were singing stars picked by eager producers according to looks; musical ability was a secondary consideration.

Dozens of starry-eyed hopefuls were always on hand. After training (Fabian, for instance, had two years of voice and etiquette lessons before cutting a record), a handful became stars, including Bobby Rydell, Neil Sedaka, Gene Pitney, Frankie Avalon, Ricky Nelson, Pat Boone, and Paul Anka. Although some aspired to the rebellious attitude of the early Elvis, most were squeaky clean and guaranteed not to offend parents.

Teen idols did not always seek out original material to sing. Sometimes, they

Teen idol Pat Boone made a career out of recording cleaned-up versions of R&B tunes.

bread covers was Pat Boone; his versions of songs like Little Richard's "Tutti Frutti" and Fats Domino's "Ain't That a Shame" had none of the energy of the originals, but they far outsold them.

Most teen idols were male and white. Exceptions to the gender barrier were Connie Francis, Brenda Lee, and ex-Mouseketeer Annette Funicello. An exception to the color barrier, meanwhile, was Chubby Checker, a black pop singer who built an entire career around a dance craze called the Twist.

The teen idol mini-industry was headquartered in Philadelphia, Pennsylvania, not coincidentally also the home of *American Bandstand*, a wildly popular daily television show that featured teens dancing to the latest hit tunes. *Bandstand*, hosted by the uncannily youthful Dick Clark, played an important role in promoting new songs (as well as dance styles and individual performers) on a national basis.

A fast-paced scene grew up around *Bandstand* and the teen idols. Producer Phil Spector, who served an apprenticeship in the Philadelphia pop mills, recalls the atmosphere:

simply recorded cleaned-up, solidly square versions of hits by rockers and black R&B artists. The king of these so-called white-

"Marvelous Teen Dreams"

In The Rolling Stone History of Rock and Roll, *writer Nik Cohn comments on Phil Spector's records.*

"No question; his records were the loudest, fiercest, most magnificent explosions that rock had yet produced, or dreamed of . . . . He stole from every source he could — Wagner, Leonard Bernstein, Broadway shows, a thousand or a million other singles, past and present — and was still completely original."

Dick Clark's popular TV show, American Bandstand, *was an integral part of promoting new songs, artists and dances.*

Philadelphia was just the most insane, most dynamite, the most beautiful city in the history of rock and roll and the world . . . . Everyone you met was raging and racing, 24 hours a day, seven days a week, and existed for nothing but hype. They existed to pull strokes, conjure deals out of nowhere, juggle hits off nothing. Money was a lot of it, of course, but there was something else as well, a real glee involved; a purist's love of hustle for its own sake.[24]

The Brill Building

The Philly scene, as Spector's characterization implies, was based on shoddy productions that were ground out quickly for a fast buck. A different ethic was at work in the Brill Building, however, located at 1619 Broadway in the heart of Manhattan's music district.

Dozens of music-related companies had (and still have) their offices in this neighborhood. During the early 1960s the Brill Building alone listed 165 such businesses in its directory. The building was, in particular, home to one remarkable group of songwriters.

The Brill Building writers became synonymous with a merger between the professionalism of older styles of pop music (such as Broadway show tunes) with the energy of the new. Many rockers were recording old standards or poor-quality originals, and few were writing their own material. The Brill Building writers set out to raise the standard, emphasizing memorable melodies and simple but sophisticated lyrics.

These writers were typically steeped in established commercial styles. But they were also relatively young, which meant that they understood teens better than old-guard songwriters. In short, they knew how to respect the traditions of conventional pop—and they knew how to rock.

They also broke the traditional barriers dictating that writing, producing, and performing were separate tasks for different groups. Often the Brill Building writers not only composed a song but also arranged the music, matched material to singer, picked backing musicians, and supervised recording sessions.

Pairs

Among the best of the Brill Building writers were three pairs of husband-wife teams: Gerry Goffin and Carole King, Jeff Barry and Ellie Greenwich, and Barry Mann and Cynthia Weil.

Goffin and King were typical. They wrote hundreds of tunes during their career together, banging out several a day on an upright piano in a tiny cubicle in a Brill Building office. While some are best forgotten ("Let's Turkey Trot"), dozens of others became enduring hits, including "Up on the Roof," "Will You Love Me Tomorrow?" and "The Loco-Motion."

The Shirelles' magnificent recording of the Goffin-King song "Will You Love Me Tomorrow?" was the first number-one song by a so-called girl group when it was released in 1960. The Shirelles were typical of the girl groups (also including the Chiffons, Chantels, Ronettes, and Shangri-Las) that were among the most popular groups to record Brill Building–style songs.

Two more sets of New York songwriters were closely associated with the Brill Building. Doc Pomus and Mort Shuman wrote dozens of classics, including "Save the Last Dance for Me," "A Mess of Blues," and "Viva Las Vegas," that were hits for Ray Charles, the Drifters, Dion, Elvis Presley, and many other artists. "Teenager in Love," originally a hit for Dion, inspired so many covers that at one point there were three different versions at the same time on the British charts.

Cubicle Rock

In The Rolling Stone History of Rock and Roll, *songwriter Barry Mann recalls the days he spent in the Brill Building with his wife and writing partner Cynthia Weil.*

"It was insane. Cynthia and I would be in this tiny cubicle, about the size of a closet, with just a piano and a chair; no window or anything. We'd go in every morning and write songs all day. In the next room Carole [King] and Gerry [Goffin] would be doing the same thing, and in the next room after that Neil [Sedaka] or somebody else. Sometimes when we all got to banging on our pianos you couldn't tell who was playing what. . . . The competition and the pressure, I suppose brought out the best in us."

Jerry Leiber and Mike Stoller, meanwhile, worked with artists ranging from blueswoman Willie Mae Thornton to Elvis Presley, although their longest collaboration was with the Coasters. Leiber and Stoller's witty songs displayed a deep understanding of both black music and the demands of commercial pop; among their hits were "Hound Dog," "Yakety Yak," and "Jailhouse Rock." Leiber and Stoller were also pioneers in a practice that is now common: near-total control of product, masterminding records from conception through production and distribution.

"Is It *Stupid* Enough?"

Philadelphia and the Brill Building both served as early training grounds for the writer-producer who is generally acknowledged as modern pop music's first boy genius.

Phil Spector was a frail Jewish kid from the Bronx who, even as a teen, displayed a gift for capturing the essence of an emotion in a few lines of song. Just out of high school he wrote "To Know Him Is to Love Him," inspired by the epitaph on his father's grave. Sung by Spector and his group, the Teddy Bears, it became a top-ten hit.

At nineteen Spector was running errands and soaking up knowledge at the Brill Building when his break came: Atlantic, a small but influential R&B label, chose a song Spector had written with an established pro, Jerry Leiber. Recorded by Ben E. King, "Spanish Harlem" was a huge hit, and from then on the kid could do no wrong.

With his own label, Philles, formed in 1962, Spector racked up an astonishing twenty hits in three years. These classic pop songs, including "And Then He Kissed Me," "Be My Baby," "You've Lost That Lovin' Feeling," and "Da Doo Ron Ron," were sung by a stable of artists, including Darlene Love, the Crystals, and the Ronettes, whose lead singer also became Spector's wife.

Brilliant at making records and at selling them, Spector was a millionaire by age twenty-one. At the height of his fame and fortune, however, he began sinking into eccentric reclusiveness.

He grew fanatical about privacy, maintained bodyguards at all times, wore dark shades and carried a gun inside, and threw tantrums if things did not go his way. He grew increasingly tyrannical about controlling every detail of his operation, from a vocalist's phrasing to publicity artwork, letterhead design, even the color of his office toilet paper. There were also reports that he abused his wife.

When one of his records flopped ("River Deep—Mountain High" by Ike and Tina Turner), Spector abruptly announced his retirement. It was 1966, and he was not quite twenty-six. Spector has since maintained his reputation as rock's Howard Hughes—a wealthy, erratic genius who made his mark before retreating into a private, exclusive world.

The Spector sound was lush and orchestral, a "wall of sound" formed by simultaneous recording of multiples of instruments: three pianos, five guitars, a set of drummers, full string sections, and so on, all pounding away behind the vocalists. Spector often called the resulting overpowering roar "little symphonies for the kids." Sonny Bono, then one of Spector's assistants, recalled: "He used to listen over and over to a new song, and he'd say,

Songwriting Changes

Ed Ward, in this excerpt from Rock of Ages, *comments on the changes in songwriting practices from the Brill Building days to more modern times.*

"From the start of the pop music industry in this country, it was the song that counted, because the artist almost never wrote his or her own material. Even as great a composer as Duke Ellington was pitched songs, and in old trade magazines, the Top Ten would feature songs, not particular versions, which would be turned out by a dozen different artists, including all the major vocalists of the day. Jukeboxes would carry the most popular songs in three or four renditions. It's hard to grasp this, in the post-Beatle era, this age of writer-composers, but it was the way the business worked until the early 1960s, when writer-composers, not the industry, first came to control their own material."

'Is it *stupid* enough, Sonny? Is it *stupid* enough?' What he meant was, is it so simple and direct and universal that *anybody* could get it?"[25]

The Birth of Top Forty

Rock and roll was changing and becoming slicker—and so was radio, the primary medium for broadcasting it.

A radio programmer's job is to make sure listeners stay tuned in. The worst thing that can happen to a programmer is for a listener to get bored and change stations. The main reason for changing stations, according to surveys, is simply hearing a poor song.

In 1957 Todd Storz, the owner of several midwestern stations, took this to its logical conclusion. One evening in a bar,

Storz noticed that the customers were playing the same forty-odd songs over and over on the jukebox. He also noticed that at the end of the evening, the waitresses—who had been hearing the songs throughout their shifts—used tip money to play the same songs yet again.

Storz thought this phenomenon might translate to radio. Would listeners stay with a format that had a playlist of only the most popular songs? Bill Drake, another pioneer in "formatted" radio, remarks, "It stands to reason. If you're playing the thirty-fifth worst record in town and somebody else is playing the eighty-seventh worst record in town, you're better off than they are."[26]

Storz tried his idea out with a station in Omaha, Nebraska. KOWH's disc jockeys played the forty most popular songs of the moment, interspersed with fast, frequent jingles and advertisements. The top-forty format proved so popular that it was adopted by other Storz-owned stations, with other radio chains following suit. Chains of stations owned by one company were becoming more common, so it was easy for multiple stations to adopt a new format at the same time.

Not everyone loved the idea, though. A number of disc jockeys resigned rather than have someone else tell them what songs they could play. For musicians, the net effect was also negative; a few songs would become smash hits, but a tightened radio market made it even more difficult than before for a noncommercial song to find success.

Payola

The nation's most prominent disc jockey, Alan Freed, continued to prosper as rock and roll spread. His sponsorship of rock-and-roll concerts was proving successful. A new job with top-rated WINS in New York City came with a then-impressive salary of seventy-five thousand dollars a year.

Unfortunately, Freed also became the center of a long-running controversy. The scandal was over unethical practices in the promotion of songs. These practices, called payola, took the form of payment (usually gifts or cash) in return for "plugging" a record—that is, giving it radio airplay.

Payola, in one form or another, had been part of radio for years; program directors and DJs routinely supplemented their salaries with "consultant fees," gifts of liquor or televisions, female companionship, and even credits on records that gave them songwriting royalties. Disc jockey "Cousin" Brucie Morrow recalls, "'Booze,

Producer Phil Spector, who developed the "wall of sound" recording style, was a millionaire by age twenty-one.

broads, whatever you want'—this was a standard offer."[27]

Many politicians and parents felt that payola itself was responsible for the popularity of rock and roll. The music was just faddish junk, they argued; the only reason teenagers listened to it was because they were being tricked into liking it by greedy, payola-taking DJs. If payola was eliminated, they felt, the music would die a natural death.

In 1959 the issue became front-page news when a congressional committee agreed to look into it.

Defenders of payola argued that the practice had been standard for years, long before the advent of rock and roll. They pointed out that the president of the Federal Communications Commission (FCC), the body that oversees radio and television, had recently accepted a free vacation in Florida from a television network.

Dick Clark was one of the central figures in what became known as the Payola Scandal. Payola was a bribe paid to disc jockeys to promote specific musicians and songs.

Small record labels also argued that payola was their only means of ensuring airplay for records since big labels could afford better distribution and promotion. While payola had its unsavory aspects, they argued, it also did good. As rock historian John Tobler writes, "On the face of it, payola did seem corrupt . . . but it did bring many great records, usually on small labels, to the public's attention."[28]

At the congressional hearings several record executives and disc jockeys confessed to accepting payola. Two of the most prominent figures under investigation were Dick Clark, the host of *American Bandstand,* and Alan Freed.

Clark was involved financially in several music-related companies, including record labels, publishing houses, and management agencies. Critics charged that these formed an obvious conflict of interest since Clark was able to boost songs that would benefit him.

Although Clark testified that he had never consciously plugged any song in which he had a financial stake, he was forced to choose between his show and his interests in music-related firms. Clark gave up the latter. His reputation was cleared and he continued to host his show.

Freed did not fare as well. He was fired from his job after refusing to agree to a similar deal. A long legal battle followed; in 1960 Freed eventually pleaded guilty to commercial bribery. Four years later he came under fire again for income tax evasion. Broke, publicly humiliated and emotionally ruined, Freed died early in 1965 at the age of forty-three.

In the eyes of many observers, Freed had been unfairly singled out. According to critic and historian Robert Palmer,

> Alan Freed was undoubtedly made the scapegoat for rock and roll's sins, real and imagined. Of course he had accepted record company payments in exchange for playing records; was there a major-league disc jockey who hadn't? Arrangements of this sort were . . . commonplace.[29]

The early sixties, despite pockets of excellence and a growing diversity, was a sluggish period for pop music. The payola scandal, meanwhile, had not helped the music's reputation among parents, politicians, and authorities.

What was needed was a shot in the arm, a jolt of new energy. When it came, it arrived from a surprising source: across the ocean.

4 The British Invasion

The guitar's all very well, John, but you'll never make a living out of it.

— John Lennon's Aunt Mimi

They've got everything over there. What do they want us for?

— Paul McCartney, en route to the first Beatles appearances in America, 1964

On February 9, 1964, an estimated 70 million Americans tuned into the *Ed Sullivan Show*, the nation's most popular television show. It was the largest audience in history for a television entertainment show. In the live theater audience were 700 people chosen from over 50,000 applicants.

Sullivan's show that night was the first American volley of the amazing phenomenon called Beatlemania. Beatlemania was a huge and unexpected tidal wave that touched off an even larger upheaval in pop music. The bands of the British Invasion reintroduced audiences to the roots of rock, bringing a fresh perspective to the blues and R&B they had loved from afar.

Their freshness and energy was a needed antidote to the faceless teen idols. Furthermore, the abundant gifts of the Beatles—especially the band's chief song-writers and singers, John Lennon and Paul McCartney—set a new standard for future generations of rock music. They were the first major band, for instance, to write most of their own material and to play a significant role in producing their own records.

To some the advent of the Beatles signaled the change of the music from old-style rock and roll to something quite different. Critic Jon Landau writes, "The Beatles shattered the dreariness of the music business. And with them came rock . . . a music quite different from rock 'n' roll."[30]

The Beatles in England

Liverpool, a tough blue-collar town in northwestern England, was an unlikely but powerful breeding ground for the Beatles. Although isolated to a degree from mainstream British culture, as a major port city it had a direct pipeline to American pop culture; sailors eagerly brought in the latest American records, which were unavailable in most of England, and a lively underground of rockers thrived in the city.

Lennon, McCartney, guitarist George Harrison, and drummer Ringo Starr were part of this subculture: four scruffy lads

The Beatles, seen here with Ed Sullivan, took the influence of American stars like Elvis Presley, Little Richard, and Chuck Berry and created an innovative new sound. They were the shot in the arm that rock and roll needed to break out of the dull dreariness of the teen idol era.

linked by a shared love of American music. The rebel stance of Elvis Presley, the weird passion of Little Richard, the clever wit of Chuck Berry, and the sweet harmonies of the Everly Brothers spoke straight to their hearts. As McCartney later recalled, "Every time I felt low I just put on an Elvis [record] and I'd feel great, beautiful. . . . 'All Shook Up'! Oh, it was beautiful!"[31]

The Beatles slowly forged a high-powered, crowd-pleasing stage act in the "beat clubs" of Liverpool and of Hamburg, Germany, another tough port city. A canny manager, Brian Epstein, then steered them toward a more polished stage act, trading in their greasy hair and leather jackets for the matching suits and "Beatle cuts" that became their trademarks.

Hard work on Epstein's part also won the band a recording contract, and its first singles took England by storm. Soon the Beatles were headlining a gruelling series of road shows, making appearances on the top television programs, and dodging increasingly large crowds of rabid fans.

The audiences of screaming teenagers who swooned over the Fab Four shocked and concerned the generally reserved British public. At the same time, Britons were charmed by the band's genuine wit and obvious talents. A comment by London's *Daily Mirror* newspaper was typical: "You have to be a real sour square not to love the nutty, noisy, happy, handsome Beatles. If they don't sweep your blues away, brother, you're a lost cause."[32]

The Beatles in America

Success in England, however, did not guarantee success in the States. No British act had ever made a dent in the American pop charts, and early efforts to release Beatles records in America had met with dismal failure. Even after the group's British successes, the president of Capitol Records (the American subsidiary of their label) told their producer, George Martin, "We

Beatlemania

David P. Szatmary, in this passage from Rockin' in Time, *elaborates on the wild commercial aspect of Beatlemania.*

"By the time the Beatles had left New York for London on February 16, the entire nation had been afflicted with Beatlemania. Headlines in the staid *Billboard* told the story: 'The U.S. Rocks and Reels from Beatles Invasion'; 'Chicago Flips Wig, Beatles and Otherwise'; 'New York City Crawling with Beatlemania'; and 'Beatle Binge in Los Angeles.' During their brief stay, the Beatles sold over 2 million records and more than $2.5 million worth of Beatle-related goods: blue and white Beatle hats; Beatle T-shirts and beach shirts; Beatle tight-fitting pants; Beatle pajamas and three-button tennis shirts; Beatle cookies; Beatle eggcups; Beatle rings, pendants, and bracelets; a pink, plastic Beatle guitar with the pictures of the four lads stamped on it; a plethora of Beatle dolls—inflatable figurines, six-inch hard rubber likenesses, painted wood dolls that bobbed their heads when moved, and a cake decoration in the form of the Beatles; Beatle nightshirts; countless Beatle publications; Beatle ice-cream sandwiches covered with a foil Beatle wrapper; Beatle soft drinks; and Beatle wigs, which Lowell Toy Company churned out at fifteen thousand a day. Seltaeb (Beatles spelled backwards), the American arm of the Beatle manufacturing giant, NEMS, even drew up plans for a Beatle motor scooter and a Beatle car."

The Beatles led the first wave of the British Invasion in 1964.

don't think the Beatles will do anything in this market."[33]

Through a fluke, however, an American disc jockey received a copy of a British single, "She Loves You." After he began playing it, its popularity spread from regional hit to nationwide smash. Capitol hastily arranged to release it in America and launched a fast publicity campaign (including large quantities of Beatle wigs) prior to their debut on the *Ed Sullivan Show.*

American critical reaction to the Beatles was mixed. The *New York Herald-Tribune* complained that they were "75% publicity, 20% haircut and 5% lilting lament." The *Washington Post* called them "asexual and homely."[34] Religious leaders and other authorities, meanwhile, considered Beatlemania just another aspect of rock and roll's moral degeneracy.

But the public's response was what counted, and in this the band triumphed. The concerts were record-breaking sensations. *Newsweek* gave them a cover story, and sales of records and merchandise rocketed. There were even dozens of tribute records—songs with titles like "We Love You Beatles," "My Boyfriend Got a Beatle Haircut," and "Ringo for President." Rock critic David P. Szatmary summarizes: "From almost every standpoint, the Beatles' visit to America had been the nine most incredible and intense days in rock and roll history."[35]

The publicity campaign, the sheer quality of the band's musicianship, and their personal charm were only some of the factors in the band's success in America. Another was their exotic nature: no American had ever heard a rock and roll band from overseas.

A final factor was a fluke of timing. In early 1964, America was a nation rocked by murder. The assassination of President John F. Kennedy in November 1963 had shaken the country to its core; all through the winter Americans had been wrapped in shock, grief, and disbelief. Finally ready for some light news, they found Beatlemania was the perfect answer. Noting how the nation's mood lifted in the wake of Beatlemania, critic Lester Bangs writes, "In retrospect, it seems obvious that this elevation of our mood had to come from outside."[36]

The Invasion Begins

Suddenly, American teens wanted to know everything about England—and to hear as much British music as possible. Groups from England suddenly found themselves the objects of rabid interest, and record companies began scrambling to find other bands that showed promise. As rock historian John Tobler writes, "Fearful of losing out on similar talent, the record companies swooped on [cities like] Liverpool, signing up anything that moved."[37]

The willy-nilly signing meant that the quality varied wildly. From Liverpool came a number of pleasant but not outstanding bands, including Gerry and the Pacemakers, Billy J. Kramer and the Dakotas, and the Swinging Blue Jeans. Another scruffy city, Manchester, yielded everything from a fine close-harmony vocal band, the Hollies, to the deeply mediocre Freddie and the Dreamers.

Some bands were little more than British-style teen idols, such as Herman's Hermits. Others were essentially amateurs, like the endearingly crude Dave Clark Five. But some were outstanding: the Spencer Davis Group's claim to fame was a soulful teenage singer, Stevie Winwood. The Animals had a hit with a raw version of an unlikely song, "House of the Rising Sun," an old blues tune about a place of prostitution. And the Kinks combined the recklessness of rock and roll with the more genteel values of middle-class England.

The Blues Return

Many British musicians were dedicated to playing pure blues and R&B, unencumbered by pop notions. Some were genuinely talented; others were earnest but hopeless. Sonny Boy Williamson, a grizzled American bluesman, reportedly returned from a tour of England in which he was backed by eager young Britons and commented, "Those English boys want to play the blues so bad. And they play it *so bad.*"[38]

The feisty British blues movement saw itself as carrying on a deep tradition, quite separate from more commercial, pop-oriented invasion music. Van Morrison, the Irish mystic poet-singer who came to prominence during the Invasion years as the leader of the R&B band Them, remarks, "The R&B movement over here was actually an antiestablishment stance. . . . It was in no shape or form meant to be a commercial entity at all."[39]

The best-known of these R&B bands eventually rose in fame to rival the Beatles. The Rolling Stones were the nasty, bad-boy flip side of the Beatles' upbeat, essentially sunny philosophy. An often-quoted comparison, attributed to writer Tom Wolfe, was that the Beatles wanted to hold your hand. . . but the Stones wanted to burn your town down. Critic Geoffrey Stokes adds, "The Beatles were *too* popular—after *A Hard Day's Night* even adults liked them

Tin Speakers

Pete Townshend of the Who, in a piece for Rolling Stone *reprinted in* The Penguin Book of Rock and Roll Writing, *offers this reminiscence of listening to rock and roll as an impressionable teen in London.*

"We, I repeat, believed only in singles. In England albums were what you got for Christmas, singles were what you bought for prestige. It was the whole re-creation of the local dancehall-cum-discotheque in your own sweet front room. You had to have the regulation tin speaker record-player, tin, not twin, housed artistically in a vinyl-covered box under a lid with a two-watt amplifier worthy only of use as a baby alarm, and a record deck on which the current Top 20 singles could be stacked twelve or fifteen high for continuous dancing of the latest dance—which differed only from last week's in the tiniest possible hip-waggling details."

The direct contrast to the bright, up-tempo Beatles was another British band called the Rolling Stones. Whereas the Beatles were relatively non-threatening, the Rolling Stones actively cultivated their image as the bad boys of rock and roll.

a little—while the scruffy Stones offered the same satisfactions a screaming Little Richard once had."[40]

Taking their name from a song by bluesman Muddy Waters, they began making the London blues scene in the early 1960s. It was an exciting time, as band member Keith Richards explains:

> When I was fifteen, rock & roll was a brand-new thing, and we were very conscious that we were in, like, a new era. . . . The world was black-and-white, and then suddenly it went into living color. Suddenly there was a reason to be around, besides just knowing you were gonna have to work and draggin' your ass to school every day.[41]

Can't Get No . . .

In the summer of 1963 the Stones recorded their first single, a cover of Chuck Berry's "Come On," that was a mod-

est success. The follow-up, "I Wanna Be Your Man," was written for them by the promising songwriting duo of Lennon and McCartney.

The band members came from a mixed background. Some were working-class lads (bassist Bill Wyman's dad was a bricklayer, drummer Charlie Watts's dad was a truck driver) while others had different backgrounds (guitarist Keith Richards attended art school, multi-instrumentalist Brian Jones grew up in a cultured and musical family, and singer Mick Jagger was once a student at the London School of Economics). The common thread was their interest in music.

Guided by manager Andrew Loog Oldham, the Stones' popularity grew as they became increasingly notorious; one memorable headline in a music magazine ad read, "Would You Let Your Daughter Go with a Rolling Stone?" The band was slow to catch on, however—especially in the American market, where it really mattered. For two years they failed to score a number-one single there, with that honor going instead to mediocre pop-oriented British bands like Peter and Gordon, Freddie and the Dreamers, and Wayne Fontana and the Mindbenders.

The Stones' breakthrough did not arrive until the summer of 1965, but it was a doozy. "Satisfaction," with its suggestive lyrics, attitude-drenched vocals, and wickedly memorable guitar riff, shot instantly to number one on both sides of the Atlantic. The song, written by Jagger and Richards, catapulted the Stones from cult band to celebrity. The group was on its way to laying claim to its later boast of being "the world's greatest rock and roll band."

Talkin' 'bout My Generation

Another Invasion band with lasting power was the Who, from a working-class neighborhood of London called Shepherd's Bush.

Originally the High Numbers, the Who was closely associated with a teen movement in England called the Mods. Mods were devoted to extremely particular fashions: exactly the right sort of scarves, shoes, shirts, anoraks (parkas), and so on. They rode motor scooters festooned with mirrors and other accessories. The right sorts of pills, usually amphetamines, were also essential; and, of course, the right bands.

As with other youth movements, this uniformity provided great comfort and sustenance to teens who felt left out of mainstream society. Pete Townshend, the Who's guitarist, songwriter, and leader, elaborates:

It was the first move I have ever seen in the history of youth towards unity, towards unity of thought, unity of drive and unity of motive. Any kid, however ugly or however f———up, if he had the right haircut and the right clothes and the right motorbike, he was a Mod. He was a Mod![42]

The sworn enemies of the Mods were Rockers, working-class teens who modeled themselves after Teddy Boys, tough motorcycle gangs that had proliferated in England in the early 1950s. They wore leather jackets, sunglasses, greasy hair, tight pants, and pointed boots called roach-stompers. The best-known British band of all, the Beatles, had been dyed-in-the-wool Rockers before their manager cleaned them up.

The Who's sound was hard and furious, and its stage attitude was one of taking no prisoners. Of the band's first hit, "My Generation," Townshend remarks, "It repulsed those it was supposed to repulse, and it drew a very thick line between the people that dug it and the people that wouldn't dig it."[43]

Though Roger Daltrey's vocals were prominent, the band's signature sound was twofold. One aspect was Townshend's choppy, crashing chording, a combination of lead and rhythm guitar playing heavily influenced by Steve Cropper of the Memphis soul band Booker T and the MGs.

The Who's other primary sound was the drumming of wild man Keith Moon, whose explosive style sometimes seemed nearly psychotic in its energy. Rock critic Geoffrey Stokes, noting that Moon's playing has influenced countless others, writes, "Moon redefined the drummer's art; after him, keeping time would be necessary but not sufficient."[44]

The Who, with their distinctive hairstyles and clothing, epitomized what was known as the Mod style.

"You Want to Bet?"

The Who's sound was not the only aspect of the band that influenced later groups. They were also pioneers of reckless habits that would become common practice among later bands.

They had legendary fights with others but especially among themselves. They inaugurated a habit of hard partying while on tour and a tradition of trashing hotel rooms. When an interviewer in later years stated to drummer Keith Moon, "You can't have destroyed as many rooms as legend has it," Moon cheerfully replied, "You want to bet?"[45]

They also began a tradition of flamboyantly destroying their equipment as part of the show. This practice began as an accident. One evening while onstage in a small club, Townshend got carried away and accidentally hit his guitar neck on an especially low ceiling. Annoyed that the audience did not notice and react appropriately, he then proceeded to smash the guitar to pieces. Townshend comments that smashing his instrument also served to vent his anger that he could not play as well as he wanted to: "It used to frustrate me incredibly. I used to try and make up visually for what I couldn't play as a musician."[46]

The guitar smashing got the expected rise out of audiences. Moon started wrecking his drum kit as well, adding flash powder for extra effect. Soon, audiences began looking forward to it as the climax of every show.

The "high point" of the Who's instrument destruction came during an appearance on the Smothers Brothers' variety show in America in 1967. Moon added more flash powder to his drum kit than usual, and the resulting explosion was far greater than planned. Townshend's hearing was permanently damaged, a piece of metal cymbal embedded itself in Moon's leg, and actress Bette Davis, a guest on the show, fainted into the arms of another guest, actor Mickey Rooney.

"Fun, Fun, Fun"

Music in the midsixties era wasn't all British accented, though it seemed that way at times. The Fab Four and other British bands dominated the air waves and pop-culture social fabric of the times, but other sounds floated around as well.

The main American group of the era—the only serious American rival to the Beatles—was the Beach Boys, a band of close-knit relatives and family friends from suburban Hawthorne, California. Their bright, poppish songs featured close multipart harmonies and lyrics that revolved around a then-current craze for surfing (which had also inspired a brief fad for "surf music" instrumentals by bands like the Del-Tones and the Surfaris).

The Beach Boys' complex, polished records were far more sophisticated and intricately arranged than most pop music. They were masterminded by the band's brilliant but eccentric leader, singer-songwriter-arranger-producer Brian Wilson. Wilson's obsessive need for control, as well as his musical style, was reminiscent of his idol, Phil Spector, a lifelong model for the younger musician.

The Beach Boys' first national hit was the 1963 "Surfin' Safari," a bright single that grafted a Chuck Berry guitar riff to a Spector-like "wall of sound" and harmony singing modeled after fifties-style vocal groups. It was followed by more songs about Wilson's chief subjects (surfing, sweet romantic love, high school, and cars): "Surfin' U.S.A.," "Surfer Girl," "I Get Around," "Fun, Fun, Fun." These early hits established the Beach Boys as perfect symbols of the California ideal: endless summers, perfect beaches, beautiful companions, and nonstop fun.

The bands that dominated the Invasion era—the Beach Boys, the Rolling Stones, the Who, the Beatles, and dozens of others—were inspired by music that was essentially black, yet they were, without exception, white. As white artists transformed R&B and blues into rock and roll, black performers were developing and refining their own modifications of the musical source material. Black popular music reached one of its most creative peaks in the mid-1960s, as it evolved into the music commonly called soul.

5 That Sweet Soul Music

Every experience I've had—good and bad—has taught me something. I was born a poor boy in the South, I'm black, I'm blind, I once fooled around with drugs, but all of it was like going to school—and I've tried to be a good student. I don't regret a damn thing.

— Ray Charles

Several vibrant new strains of black music began developing out of R&B before and during the period when the British Invasion returned pop music to its roots. Typified by a handful of distinctive performers and regional styles, these strains were known collectively as soul music.

Soul was closely allied with the political and social climate of the times, specifically the strides that black citizens were making in the sixties to assert their civil rights and racial identity. It was a hopeful time for many, full of promise and pride, and the music's essentially joyous nature reflected this.

Like the blues, soul contained a potent mixture of sadness and joy, but more often than not it emphasized the positive. According to American music historian Peter Guralnick,

It was a peculiarly good-hearted and optimistic sort of music, and it is no accident that its popularity was limited to the early and middle Sixties, a time when awakening black pride went hand in hand with civil rights activism and racial progress seemed more real than illusory.[47]

Even more dramatically than other forms of rock and roll, soul's roots can be traced directly to the sacred music of the black church. Indeed, many popular soul artists, including Sam Cooke, Aretha Franklin, and Clyde McPhatter of the Drifters, first gained fame as gospel singers.

Brother Ray

Before these singers hit their stride, however, one man was already exploring the connection between sacred and popular music. In his recordings of the late 1950s and early 1960s, Ray Charles merged the passion of gospel with more worldly forms of music, laying the groundwork for—and, some say, inventing—soul music.

Growing up poor in Florida, Ray Charles Robinson began to lose his sight at the age of six. While attending a school for the blind, he began learning piano; by age fifteen he was a professional musician, and he was completely blind.

Relocating to Seattle in 1947 (because, he says, it was as far from Florida as he could get), the young musician became a fixture in that town's black club scene, dropping his last name to avoid confusion with the boxer "Sugar" Ray Robinson. He began recording in 1949 in Los Angeles, but he did not score a hit until 1951 with "Baby, Let Me Hold Your Hand."

At this point, Charles's music was a fairly conventional brand of jazzy pop similar to that of his idol, Nat "King" Cole. Charles would not begin creating truly original music until Atlantic Records signed him in 1954.

The New York R&B label was relatively small but had a loyal and fanatical following. Atlantic cared less about making commercial "product" than about giving its artists free rein to develop individual styles. Thus, Atlantic let Charles choose his own material, sidemen, arrangements, and even production style.

The result was a groundbreaking combination. On top of a gospel-based song structure and a rolling, churchy piano, Charles added his own powerful vocals and backup singers straight out of the church's classic call-and-response choir. Charles's best records had a high-spirited, fierce earthiness familiar to fans of gospel music but shockingly direct in the world of 1950s pop.

"I've Got a Woman," released in 1955, was the first of Charles's many national hits. "What'd I Say," his first million-seller, was banned by many radio stations, not for its lyrics, which were unremarkable, but for Charles's joyous moans, which were clearly suggestive of certain taboo earthly pleasures.

Not content to recycle his groundbreaking gospel-pop style, Charles left At-

Singer Ray Charles combined jazz, gospel and country to create a unique sound of his own. Because he was versatile, Charles was also known as the Genius of Soul.

lantic in 1959 for another company, ABC, which gave him even more room to experiment with a variety of styles, including country, jazz, and Broadway show tunes. This versatility was responsible for Frank Sinatra's famous comment that Charles was "the only genius in this business."

"You Send Me"

For many fans, especially white listeners, Ray Charles was a little too raw. Another gifted singer, Sam Cooke, did much to popularize gospel-tinged music for mainstream audiences.

For the first half of the 1950s, Cooke's soaring vocals made his group, the Soul Stirrers, one of the country's top gospel groups. Devout gospel fans were thus outraged when their beloved singer started making solo pop records in 1956; in fact, he was forced to use a pseudonym for the first of these.

But Cooke persevered, and his first major single, 1957's "You Send Me," was a smash hit, selling 1.7 million copies as a "crossover" song, that is, one that scored high on both pop (white) and R&B (black) charts. Its success led to a contract with RCA, a major label that until then had only one other black artist, the calypso singer Harry Belafonte. Many more hits followed, including "Chain Gang," "Twistin' the Night Away" and "Havin' a Party."

For those who found Ray Charles's music too raw, there was Sam Cooke (pictured). His warm voice had a wider appeal to fans of gospel music.

Cooke's warm vocals were a major influence on many later singers, including Otis Redding and Rod Stewart, but he stood out in another important way. He was also one of the first black pop artists to run his own publishing company, management firm, and record label. Thus, he was an important pioneer in black entrepreneurship.

Tragically, Cooke was killed in 1964, gunned down by the manager of a seedy Los Angeles motel after he had allegedly assaulted a young woman. His last single, "A Change Is Gonna Come," was released just after his death. It is a stately, yearning plea for racial equality, nearly as moving as another central text in the civil rights movement, Martin Luther King Jr.'s famous "I Have a Dream" speech.

The Hardest-Working Man in Show Business!

A third cornerstone of soul was the amazing James Brown, variously known as the Hardest-Working Man in Show Business, Mr. Dynamite, the Godfather of Soul, and Soul Brother Number One.

Born in Macon, Georgia, Brown spent his early years shining shoes and picking cotton. He also spent time in reform school and flirted with being a professional boxer and baseball player before turning to music full-time.

Brown's gift lay in settling into extended grooves and using a static but hypnotic set of chords in seemingly endless repetition. The singer, the band's drummers (there were two), and the horn section would bounce complex, inventive rhythms and riffs off a rock-steady guitar and bass. Brown's music was funk before the term *funk* came into general use.

In Brown's setup, as in traditional African music, rhythm was everything, and his musicians learned to watch carefully for the leader's subtle hand and body gestures signaling rhythmic changes. (In fact, they were docked pay if they missed cues.) Brown's road manager, Alan Leeds, remarks that the net effect wove a complex patchwork: "So the magic became something like putting a quilt together—taking all the rhythm patterns and weaving them in such a magical way as to create this wonderful *feel* that's going to drive audiences crazy."[48]

Though Brown had a number of hit singles, the time constraints of a typical three-minute single could not capture his extended grooves adequately on disc. Long-playing albums were his medium, and in 1963 an album of a live performance at New York's Apollo Theater spent sixty-six weeks on the *Billboard* sales charts—an astonishing feat for any singer, especially someone as uncommercially gritty as Brown.

In the years since, Brown's grainy voice, mind-bending dance steps, flashy stage show, and, above all, revolutionary sense of rhythm have deeply moved performers as recent as rap and hip-hop artists. "There should be a statue of him in every park in America," Chrissie Hynde of the Pretenders states. "He had the greatest influence of anyone in contemporary music."[49]

The Memphis Sound

To many fans sultry Memphis, Tennessee, with its long history as a center for blues

James Brown, also known as the Godfather of Soul, was known for weaving complex grooves and rhythms into a unique form of soul that was the precursor to funk music.

and R&B, is the most soulful city in the world. During the sixties one of the most important strains of soul came from Memphis's Stax Records.

The Stax style—grittier than most pop, but appealing to both black and white audiences—was the product of a single cozy studio and its collection of ancient machines constantly on the verge of breaking down. Stax's stable of house producers, writers, singers, and musicians provided a distinctive and cohesive sound for the label's output while individual singers made each record stand out.

One thing that set Stax apart was that its core team of producers, engineers, and musicians was racially mixed. The band on dozens of Stax hits was the multiracial Booker T and the MGs, famed for their precision-crafted rhythms and riffs. Aiding the MGs was another racially mixed team, the Memphis Horns.

Virtually all of Stax's solo artists, meanwhile, were black. Among the most successful were the duo of Sam and Dave ("Soothe Me," "Soul Man," "When Something Is Wrong with My Baby"), Carla Thomas ("Gee Whiz"), Eddie Floyd ("Knock on Wood"), and Wilson Pickett, whose many hits included "(In the) Midnight Hour" and "Mustang Sally."

The Memphis singer many consider the greatest of them all had a tragically short career. Otis Redding was blessed with a voice halfway between the silky charm of Sam Cooke and the coarse urgency of James Brown, and he was also a gifted songwriter. Among his enduring self-penned hits were "Mr. Pitiful," "Respect" (recorded by Redding before Aretha Franklin did her famous version) and "(Sittin' on) The Dock of the Bay."

On the verge of international stardom, Redding and several members of his touring band were killed in an airplane crash in 1967. His appeal and influence, which continue to this day, are summed up by MGs guitarist Steve Cropper: "He gets over to the people what he's talking about, and he does it in so few words that if you read them on paper they might not make any sense. But when you hear the way he sings them, you know exactly what he is talking about."[50]

Don't Forget the Motor City

Far to the north of Memphis, in the blue-collar automotive center of Detroit, Michigan, another important sound was forming.

Detroit, the Motor City, was the birthplace of Motown Records, the most spectacularly successful black-owned music organization in history. The Motown story developed parallel to the civil rights movement, and it was a model of the movement's ideals of self-determination, inclusiveness, and achievement. Rock historian Paul Friedlander writes that Motown was "a Black economic civil rights parable for the sixties."[51]

Like the ramshackle Stax studios, the modest building that housed Motown Records was an unlikely site for the production of timeless music. But with typical confidence and enthusiasm, early on founder Berry Gordy put a sign over the door that announced "Hitsville, U.S.A."

This bravado was, over the years, justified. As critic Ed Ward writes, "In an age when a youthful President [Kennedy] was setting the style for the nation, Gordy . . . proclaimed the music on his records 'The Sound of Young America,' and judging from the numbers in which they sold, nobody was likely to contradict him."[52]

Motown's first two big sellers in 1960 were radically different: Barrett Strong's raucous "Money" featured the singer's gravelly voice and a straight-shooting lyric ("Money! That's what I want!"). In contrast, "Shop Around" by Smokey Robinson and the Miracles took advantage of a catchy melody and the lead singer's creamy, soothing voice.

Within a few years Gordy had assembled a remarkable stable of singers, pro-

The World's Best Car Music

Paul Friedlander, in this excerpt from Rock and Roll: A Social History, *points out the deliberate push to make Motown music sound great through tinny speakers.*

"Part of Motown's true genius was the manner in which it arranged instruments into a distinct 'sound.' [Founder Berry] Gordy had long ago recognized that most of his listeners were young and that they heard popular music either in their cars or on transistor radios. He also realized the limitations of these units: car and transistor radios produced lousy, thin sound. Thus, Motown tailored its music to overcome these limitations; certain elements in the music were emphasized while others were pushed to the background."

In the late 1950s Berry Gordy founded what was to become the most successful black music enterprise in America, Motown Records.

ducers, writers, and musicians. Like the Stax label, Motown's strategy was to back distinctly different singers with a house band that created an immediately identifiable trademark sound. Phil Spector remarks, "You put on a Motown record and it jumps at you."[53] Memphis producer Isaac Hayes adds, "What Motown did was very smart. They beat the kids over the head with it. That wasn't very soulful to us down at Stax, but baby, it *sold*."[54]

Not every Motown release was a smash; nonetheless, the label had an amazing suc-

cess rate. Throughout the 1960s over 65 percent of the label's releases reached the top one hundred; other labels were lucky to average 10 percent. The hits came with stunning rapidity: "Please Mr. Postman" by the Marvelettes, "Two Lovers" by Mary Wells, "Stubborn Kind of Fellow" by Marvin Gaye, "You've Really Got a Hold on Me" by the Miracles, "Fingertips" by eleven-year-old "Little" Stevie Wonder, "My Girl" by the Temptations—not to mention twelve number-one hits within five years for Diana Ross and the Supremes.

A Happy Family

Motown owed much of its success to streamlined techniques. Gordy modeled these on the quality control he had seen as a worker in Detroit's automobile factories. Gordy recalls, "I worked on the Ford assembly line, and I thought, 'Why can't we do that with the creative process?'"[55]

Like the assembly-line process for cars, Motown production was streamlined, with specific jobs performed by highly trained individuals. One producer, for instance, would work intensively with one vocalist instead of the casual swapping typical in pop music at the time.

The process of preparing performers for live shows was likewise closely controlled. Singers were often groomed for months before recording or appearing in public, receiving lessons in how to sit, walk, talk, and even smoke with elegance and grace. Outfits and dance steps were designed and taught by in-house experts.

Another factor in the label's success was Gordy's knack for picking gifted producers and songwriters. Smokey Robinson worked with virtually every Motown group, including his own, and was such a brilliant songwriter that he was once labeled "America's greatest living poet"[56] by no less an authority than Bob Dylan. Another writing-production team—the trio of Lamont Dozier and brothers Eddie and Brian Holland—wrote and produced twenty-eight top-twenty hits within three years, beginning with Martha and the Vandellas' "Heat Wave" in 1963.

A third factor in Motown's success was its cohesiveness. Gordy encouraged his colleagues to think of Motown as one big happy family, with himself as the father figure. Most artists were kept on allowances, with the company doling out only a small portion of their earnings and keeping the rest in trust. Critic Geoffrey Stokes comments on Gordy's business philosophy:

> The loss of freedom [to Motown's employees] was real, but so were the services Gordy provided. He expected his artists to achieve (as he had), be loyal (as his family was), and crack the racial barriers that had also stood in his way. To an astonishing degree, they did.[57]

Lady Soul

In the last years of the 1960s, a final cornerstone of soul was put in place when Aretha Franklin hit her stride.

During those glory years Lady Soul, as Franklin was called, not only represented the essence of soul music but also stood for the dream of racial unity that was central to the civil rights movement. This was demonstrated by her massive popularity with both white and black audiences and the critical praise lavished on her.

Franklin's father was a Detroit minister with a national reputation for his stirring sermons. Her first musical experiences were in his church, and she was deeply influenced by the greats of gospel, including Mahalia Jackson and Clara Ward. Even as a teenager, Franklin had a voice powerful enough to stop a train. John Hammond, who had been an influential promoter of black music for decades, pronounced her "an untutored genius, the best voice I've heard since [jazz singer] Billie Holiday."[58]

Hammond signed Franklin to Columbia Records, but executives there tried to make her into a smooth nightclub singer, backing her with an orchestra and chorus and giving her Broadway show tunes to sing. The results were disappointing, and Atlantic Records scooped her up when her Columbia contract expired in 1966.

As they had done with Ray Charles, Atlantic's executives gave Franklin artistic freedom, and within a year she was one of the most successful singers in the nation. Producer Jerry Wexler helped by suggesting she record with an obscure group of white musicians based in tiny Muscle Shoals, Alabama. Though Franklin was sceptical, Wexler convinced her that the Muscle Shoals cats were compatible.

It was a brilliant match. The musicians, deeply funky and steeped in both black and white music, were perfect foils for Franklin. Together they produced a timeless string of singles: "Respect," "Do Right Woman," "See Saw," "(You Make Me Feel Like a) Natural Woman," and many more.

To listeners used to the relatively sweet female vocalists of Stax and Motown, Franklin was a revelation. Her strength and assertiveness served as models for both the civil rights movement and the emerging feminist movement. Rock critic Peter Shapiro writes, "Her voice fused with the groove to become an object of unmovable defiance. . . . [She] demanded respect and fought for sexual equality."[59]

The classic soul music movement ended at roughly the same time as an event that marked the end of the civil rights movement: the assassination of Mar-

Aretha Franklin, known to her fans as Lady Soul, was the last major star of the classic gospel era. The daughter of a Detroit minister, she was discovered singing in her father's church.

tin Luther King Jr. in 1968. As the more assertive black power movement took the place of King's message of nonviolence, black music also changed. The generally optimistic, inclusive philosophy of soul was replaced by one that was more overtly militant and divisive.

Meanwhile, big changes were taking place in the wider world of rock and roll. As the political and social upheavals of the sixties took shape, more and more performers were exploring revolutionary new branches of the music.

6 The Sixties: Rock Explodes

Everything was changing, all these doors were being opened, and it made you think, "I could try anything, right now." Revolutionary times are very healthy for experimenting and trying stuff—and for being fearless in what you try.

—Robbie Robertson of the Band

They're paying me $50,000 a year to be like me!

—Janis Joplin

The era called the sixties actually spanned a period from roughly the mid-1960s to the early 1970s. In America and elsewhere, it was an intense time of political and social unrest characterized by volatile events: student-led protests against America's role in Vietnam and nuclear energy, the sexual revolution, the women's movement, experiments in communal living and drugs, and the assassinations of Martin Luther King Jr. and Robert Kennedy.

The era was both blissed-out and tense, a paradox reflected in its popular music. In the sixties rock underwent an astonishing period of diversity and experimentation, in keeping with the era's sense of political activism and the questioning of

established norms. Sometime during the sixties—no one is sure exactly when—rock and roll became rock. The phrase *rock and roll* came to mean the music of the classic early rockers. The newer stuff, rock, began taking itself quite seriously as musicians expanded their horizons and sought the status of legitimate artists, not just entertainers.

From Rock and Roll to Just Rock

As the freedom available to rockers expanded, new and exotic styles sprouted up everywhere, along with exotic instruments and studio effects. Anything from Indian ragas to jazz riffs could be blended into the mix. Lyrics quoted the Tibetan Book of the Dead and obscure French poets. As never before, musicians also began to write their own songs, produce their own records, even organize their concerts and develop new record labels.

Rock could flourish in this way because it was no longer a quick fad: It was without a doubt the dominant form of popular music. Therefore, record companies were willing to underwrite the increasingly expensive process of producing albums. The

Geoffrey Stokes, in his book Rock of Ages, *has this to say about how the Beatles' legacy affected later singers and composers.*

"It's important to remember how much the Beatles, Dylan, and their sixties successors shaped our expectations of popular musicians. Bobby-soxers had screamed for Sinatra, and Elvis's hips had mesmerized a nation, but no one had taken their ideas seriously—or, for that matter, cared if they had any. Even when they were. . . at their most intellectually persuasive. . . , their words came from somewhere else. The Beatles sang their own songs, spoke their own thoughts. The folkies expected this as a matter of course from a [political singer like] Phil Ochs, but this was the first time that expectation had gone national. The resulting shock wasn't because the Beatles were always intelligent or witty, but that they ever were."

first Beatles album took sixteen hours and about one thousand pounds to produce in 1963; *Sgt. Pepper,* released in 1967, required seven hundred hours and twenty-five thousand pounds.

But the return was worth the expense. Though singles still generated important sales shares, albums were quickly surpassing them as both artistic expression and as a potent commercial force. Musicians, fans, and music-industry executives alike were confident both of the music itself and of its place on the sales charts.

Listeners took the music more seriously too. High-school English teachers analyzed rock lyrics; one of the world's top classical conductors, Leonard Bernstein, hosted a television special on rock; and clergy incorporated rock into religious services. As rock criticism became a legitimate form of journalism, the music was also analyzed and considered as thoroughly as clas-sical music. It had come a long way from the days when TV host Steve Allen got laughs with a mock-dramatic reading of the rockabilly classic "Be Bop a Lula."

Sgt. Pepper Taught the Band to Play

In many ways the music of the sixties—and perhaps the sixties as a whole—can be represented by a single album.

Sgt. Pepper's Lonely Hearts Club Band hit the world like a thunderbolt when it was released smack in the middle of the Summer of Love 1967. To many fans and critics, it remains the crowning achievement by the greatest rock group of all time—the first work to successfully merge the energy of pop music with the depth of true art.

In 1967 the Beatles, considered by many to be the foremost rock band of all time, released what was considered the crowning glory of their career and sixties rock, Sgt. Pepper's Lonely Hearts Club Band.

The album's elaborate production reflected the Beatles' decision to stop touring and to concentrate on studio work. It also reflected the band's then-current interests: antiwar protests, the burgeoning psychedelic movement, Eastern music and religion, and drug experimentation. Technically, the achievements of the musicians and producer George Martin are still astonishing, especially in light of the fact that *Sgt. Pepper* was created with monaural four-track tape recorders, extremely crude machines by today's standards.

Public reaction was divided. All over the world devoted fans considered it holy scripture and searched it for hidden cosmic messages. More conservative fans bought it even if they were baffled by its psychedelic overtones (it sold a million copies in America alone within two weeks of its release). Critics were generally ecstatic; the *New York Times* hailed it as "a new and golden Renaissance of Song."[60]

On the other hand, the BBC banned the single "A Day in the Life" because of alleged drug references, and conservative groups on both sides of the Atlantic condemned the band as degenerates out to brainwash youth into drug use and dissolution.

The audience for an album like *Sgt. Pepper* spanned the world. As rock's audiences grew ever larger, and as the ability to serve those audiences with concerts and recordings grew more sophisticated, music became less regional. However, pockets of regional scene-making still existed.

If You're Going to San Francisco

Far and away the most influential of these was San Francisco. The Bay Area's laid-back college-town atmosphere, long-established tolerance of eccentricity, politicized environment, and overall bohemian image incubated a unique cultural moment in the sixties: psychedelia.

The psychedelic movement was rooted in many things: a counterculture that advocated a communal society and drugs, especially hallucinogens, as a means of freeing consciousness; a fervent belief in leftist politics and antiwar activism; a fondness for long hair and eye-popping clothes; and the conviction that New Age religion could bring the planet together in peace and harmony—or, failing that, that violent revolution was the way of the future.

Hippies, the free speech movement, free food programs, free medical clinics, the Black Panther movement—all of it came together in San Francisco. Other cities had similar cultural uprisings, but things just seemed groovier in San Francisco. As critic Geoffrey Stokes writes, "'We Shall Overcome' and the other freedom songs had a certain dignity and emotional appeal, but it was San Francisco that gave birth to the undeniably attractive idea that you could boogie your way to revolution."[61]

What a Trip

Several musical styles emerged from San Francisco, but the most innovative was psychedelia. Psychedelic music was made elsewhere—in London by Pink Floyd, for instance—but the Bay Area was psychedelia's ground zero.

It was, crudely put, an attempt to recreate the experience of a mind-altering drug trip through music; hence, its alternate name of acid rock. Psychedelic music was characterized by long improvised solos (especially by flashy lead guitarists), spacey noises, experiments in feedback, and thundering drums. The music itself was augmented by free-form dancing and light shows that seem crude by today's performance standards but were radical at the time. The overall effect was electrifying; one of the scene's seminal musicians, guitarist Jerry Garcia, once remarked, "Magic is what we do. Music is how we do it."[62]

Following early experiments by bands like the Charlatans and the Great Society, psychedelia was in full bloom by 1967. Estimates of the number of psychedelic bands in the Bay Area in that year alone range from five hundred to fifteen hundred. Most disappeared quickly, but some had lasting appeal.

Quicksilver Messenger Service and Santana both featured exceptional lead guitarists in, respectively, John Cippolina and Carlos Santana. Two unusually strong female vocalists, Grace Slick and Janis Joplin, were the forces that powered two other bands, Jefferson Airplane and Big Brother and the Holding Company. The Bay Area was also home to one of the era's most influential black musicians, Sly Stone, who fused the wild abandon of white rock with the precision of a black soul band.

But the quintessential San Francisco band was the Grateful Dead, powered by the fluid guitar of Jerry Garcia. The group was closely associated with the Acid Tests, a series of enormous free-form parties masterminded by writer Ken Kesey. The Acid Tests, inspired by the powers of LSD (which was then still legal), were blueprints for the emerging psychedelic culture; rock critic Parke Puterbaugh writes that they were "powerful, defining events that ushered in a liberated age of soul searching, drug taking, lovemaking and music unlike any heard before."[63]

Deadheads Unite

The Grateful Dead remained together far longer than most rock bands, and in their long career they came to stand for a great deal to their enormous community of devoted fans, the Deadheads. In this passage from his book Night Beat, *author and critic Mikal Gilmore comments on these hard-core fans.*

"For the Dead's fans, the band was not simply another popular phenomenon that spoke for any one certain moment, nor merely a band that achieved a temporary place of fame and commodity in the ongoing chronicle of pop music. To the group's believers, the Dead were something much bigger and more lasting, as well as something virtually unique in postwar musical history: a band that functioned as an ongoing, binding central point in a large-scale alternative music scene that viewed music as a crucial means of expressing a vision of a better, more hopeful and open-minded society."

Grateful Dead guitarist Jerry Garcia.

Guitar Gods

The guitar had long been the preeminent instrument of rock, a factor cemented in the sixties by the advent of several so-called guitar gods from England.

One was Eric Clapton, a disciple of American bluesmen. He inspired such devotion in his early days in London that a common bit of graffiti around the city read "Clapton Is God." Slowhand Clapton, as he was ironically nicknamed, spent time with the Invasion band the Yardbirds and a pioneering British blues band, John Mayall's Bluesbreakers, before forming his own band, Cream, with two other virtuosos, bassist Jack Bruce and drummer Ginger Baker. During its short life, 1966 to 1968, Cream played some of the fastest, most extended, most overpoweringly loud blues-rock in the world, typified by its double album *Wheels of Fire.*

Like Clapton, Jeff Beck also apprenticed with the Yardbirds. His solo work with the Jeff Beck Group never achieved widespread success, although its singer, Rod Stewart, found massive fame later.

Nonetheless, Beck's precisely articulated playing, more aggressive than that of Clapton's, was widely influential among other guitarists.

A third ex-Yardbirds guitarist, Jimmy Page, used the spare instrumental setup of Cream and the Jeff Beck Group for his own band, Led Zeppelin. Page's style, both ponderous and precise, become a linchpin in the later development of heavy metal, and Led Zeppelin became one of the most imitated bands in history.

The most influential sixties guitarist of all also first found fame in England, though he came from America. Jimi Hendrix was instantly, flamboyantly recognizable: he played with his teeth and behind his back, he ripped incredibly powerful licks out of the air, and he exploited feedback like no one else. Hendrix was one of rock's true originals, redefining possibilities and setting new standards.

Purple Haze

Born and raised in Seattle, Hendrix spent years backing R&B artists before going solo. He was leading a New York City blues band in 1966 when Chas Chandler of the Animals predicted he could be a star in England.

In London, Chandler hooked Hendrix up with bassist Noel Redding and drummer Mitch Mitchell. The Jimi Hendrix Experience played a freaked-out, shockingly loud version of blues-influenced rock, with a stage style favoring grand gestures and mock-Edwardian clothes as elaborate as their music. (Offstage, Hendrix was notoriously shy and withdrawn.)

The band was a sensation in Europe, and two singles, "Hey Joe" and "Purple

Haze," did well on the British charts. But Hendrix remained a rumor in America until the summer of 1967, when a stunning appearance at the Monterey International Pop Festival climaxed with the performer burning his guitar; the *Los Angeles Times* noted at the time, "When Jimi left the stage, he had graduated from rumor to legend."[64]

Hendrix's flame burned brightly but quickly: Three years after Monterey he was dead, the victim of a (probably accidental) drug overdose. But his recorded output (including *Are You Experienced?* and *Axis:*

One of the most original and influential artists of the 1960s was guitarist Jimi Hendrix. In his short career, Hendrix completely redefined guitar rock.

Bold as Love) continues to inspire musicians the world over. According to rock critic John Morthland, "Hendrix created a branch on the pop tree that nobody else has ventured too far out on. None has actually extended the directions he pursued, but perhaps that is because he took them, in his painfully short time on earth, as far as they could go."[65]

"The Times They Are A-Changin' "

Many other musical styles besides psychedelia blossomed in the sixties. Some grew out of a folk-music boom of the early sixties that emphasized political protest and social issues and was in many ways an outgrowth of the intellectual beatnik movement of the 1950s. Jim McGuinn, a key figure in the trend, recalls, "Folk music was very hip. It was . . . wearing goatees and black turtlenecks and sunglasses at night."[66]

Songs like "The Times They Are A-Changin'" and "Blowin' in the Wind" summed up, for many, folk's commitment to individual freedom and social change. The author of these songs was Robert Allen Zimmerman, the son of a Minnesota hardware store owner. Bob Dylan, as he renamed himself, became "the voice of his generation" and the premiere figure in folk music despite a nasal voice and a style that featured deliberately obscure, mysterious wordplay. When asked to define the

---

Out of Fashion

In a 1983 interview reprinted in Timothy White's book Rock Lives, *singer-songwriter Paul Simon was asked this question: Who, besides John Lennon, do you believe has been a positive inspirational figure in rock? This was his reply.*

"Dylan. He made us feel at a certain time that it was good to be smart, to be observant, that it was good to have a social conscience. These are all things that are out of fashion now. Real art remains when the fashion changes, but art can run conjunctively with fashion. Both can occasionally be quite intelligent at the same time."

Folk hero Robert Zimmerman, a.k.a. Bob Dylan.

---

term *folk music,* for instance, he once replied, "As a constitutional replay of mass production."[67]

In 1965 Dylan took a radical step, performing at the Newport Folk Festival with an electric band. The move outraged the relatively small world of purist folkies, who claimed Dylan had sold out, but it also gained him a huge new audience who realized he had created an exciting new style of music: folk with a rock beat.

Among those who went on to explore this so-called folk-rock were the Buffalo Springfield, the Lovin' Spoonful, Simon and Garfunkel, and the Mamas and the Papas. The movement touched English musicians as well, with singers like Donovan and bands like Fairport Convention mixing traditional Celtic music with rock.

Probably the most popular folk-rockers were the Byrds, who combined traditional folk and the trademark jangly sound of Jim McGuinn's twelve-string guitar with cool, sophisticated studio techniques typical of their home, Los Angeles. Their first single, "Mr. Tambourine Man," was written by Dylan; it became an enormous hit, an anthem for the era, and the Byrds' best-known song.

Dylan and the Byrds were responsible for an extension of folk-rock that explored another branch of America's roots: country music. Dylan's quiet, acoustic album *John Wesley Harding* (1967) and the sweetly corny *Nashville Skyline* (1969) featured simple, spare productions and the cleanly defined pleasures of country music. Meanwhile, the Byrds' *Sweethearts of the Rodeo* (1968) was another definitive statement of country-rock. The style was a sharp departure from Dylan's and the Byrds's previous music—and from the ornate nature of most rock of the late sixties.

Rock critic Mikal Gilmore notes that, "in effect, *John Wesley Harding* flattened the visions and ambitions of psychedelia."[68]

"Proud Mary" and *Big Pink*

Two other prominent sixties bands stayed determinedly away from the trendiness of psychedelia.

For a period in 1969–1970, a roots-oriented band from the Bay Area, one that stressed unfashionable blue-collar values and no-nonsense, unflashy songs, dominated the radio. Easily accessible to a wide audience, Creedence Clearwater Revival (CCR) churned out a steady release of top singles, including "Bad Moon Rising" and "Proud Mary." Their sound was straightforward and stripped-down, deeply influenced by rockabilly and by what singer-songwriter John Fogerty called "swamp" music.

The other band rose from obscurity when Bob Dylan selected them as his post-Newport touring band. Known at various times as the Hawks, the Crackers, and the Canadian Squires, the group (four Canadians and an American) eventually settled on being simply the Band.

Their first album, *Music from Big Pink,* appeared in mid-1968, during Dylan's long period of isolated recuperation from a motorcycle accident. The album featured a cover painting by Dylan, and some of the songs, including "I Shall Be Released," were written or cowritten by the missing master. The Dylan connection was heady stuff, but the album was stunning on its own.

Led by the terse guitar and writing of Robbie Robertson, and drawing from a deep knowledge of gospel, blues, R&B, and country, the Band evoked a sweeping vision of American music. In its eloquent simplicity, *Music from Big Pink* was a fresh and profoundly influential alternative to the convolutions of psychedelia.

Albums Ascendant

CCR and the Band exemplified some of the profound changes in the way music was marketed in the sixties. CCR was basically a singles band with a knack for producing pithy three-minute vignettes perfect for the radio. The Band, on the other hand, showed how a group that did not rely on commercial singles could still become widely popular.

Bands that relied on albums to express themselves could still find audiences and radio play, especially on so-called "underground" stations. These FM stations were less commercial-driven than AM stations, with laid-back disc jockeys who thought nothing of playing entire album sides between commercial breaks or talk.

The rise in popularity of albums and underground FM affected record-sales techniques. A Los Angeles band, the Doors, scored an enormous hit with its first single, "Light My Fire." One version was about three minutes long, the usual length for top-forty singles. But then executives at Elektra, the band's label, realized that the album version, which was over twice as long to take advantage of Jim Morrison's dark vocals and Ray Manzarek's towering organ playing, was being played more often by both underground and top-forty stations.

Elektra then heavily promoted the album, not the single. The strategy paid off:

The album rose to number two, topped only by *Sgt. Pepper*. A similar situation occured with Jimi Hendrix's first album; though neither of its two singles made much of an impact, *Are You Experienced?* sold well and reached number five on the *Billboard* charts. The rise of albums boosted rock's creativity. Rock critic Geoffrey Stokes notes that the change "opened the industry doors to a wide range of musical, intellectual, psychedelic, and role-playing experiments."[69]

Music, Love, and Flowers

One of the most galvanizing of all sixties phenomena was the rock festival. The first major rock festival was the Monterey International Pop Festival in June 1967, modeled on established festivals for jazz and folk. In keeping with the spirit of the times, performers at the California event were paid only expenses, with profits going to free clinics and music programs for needy families. The festival's motto was Music, Love, and Flowers.

For the first time Americans were exposed to live performances by Hendrix and the Who. Thanks to acts like Janis Joplin, Otis Redding, the Buffalo Springfield, Simon and Garfunkel, and the Mamas and the Papas, the event drew a far bigger crowd than anticipated: seven thousand people had tickets, but another fifty thousand showed up. Disgusted locals called it "a hippie invasion."

More festivals followed. Many were shoddily produced, however, with poor organization, inadequate sanitation, and inflated prices. Dangerous drugs were prevalent, medical facilities were often overwhelmed, and gate-crashers often provoked hostility from legitimate ticket holders. A festival in Palm Springs, California, ended in rioting and mass arrests, a rowdy Denver festival crowd was dispersed with tear gas, and one in Los Angeles created a half-million dollars in property damage.

In light of these problems, some communities banned festivals outright. Others tried to regulate them with restrictions such as huge damage deposits. Nonetheless, promoters were able to stage some memorable shows. Among these were a peace benefit in Toronto featuring John Lennon and Yoko Ono and the Isle of Wight Festival off the English coast, which headlined Bob Dylan as well as Jimi Hendrix in his last public appearance.

"Nothing *but* Fun and Music"

The most famous festival of all, the Woodstock Music and Art Fair, was not actually held in Woodstock. When organizers were forced to vacate the original site in tiny Woodstock, New York, an alternative was found on a farm in the nearby (and equally small) town of Bethel.

Woodstock, which took place in the summer of 1969, featured performers ranging from folk singers Joan Baez and Arlo Guthrie to rock musicians Jimi Hendrix, the Who, and Sly Stone. Sanitation, medical tents, and other facilities were prepared for the 150,000 people that organizers anticipated.

What no one realized was that the event would become a magnet for young music fans. Long before the music began, the festival was out of control. Enormous

In June 1967 Janis Joplin performed at the first major rock music festival, the Monterey International Pop Festival.

crowds jammed the roads around Bethel for miles. Attempts at ticket-taking had to be abandoned as hundreds of thousands of people simply came over the fences. The sound system would have been adequate for the expected crowd, but little of the music could be heard at the fringes of the enormous mass of people who showed up.

Estimates of this population range from three hundred thousand to four hundred thousand. Water, food, security, and sanitation were ridiculously inadequate for what was, temporarily, the state's third-largest city. Then, when the rain started, Woodstock became one gigantic mud puddle.

Miraculously, none of this seemed to matter very much. Considering the potential for disaster, there were few major crises. Three drug-related deaths were offset by three births. The promoters lost over a million dollars, but a documentary film about the festival more than made that back. Max Yasgur, the farmer on whose property the festival occurred, summed up Woodstock's spirit when he told a cheering crowd, "You are the largest group of people ever assembled in one place at one time . . . and you have proven something to the world . . . that half a million kids can get together for fun and music and have nothing *but* fun and music."[70]

Altamont

Later that year an event occurred that was in many ways the opposite of "nothing *but* fun and music."

A free concert by the Rolling Stones at the Altamont Speedway, near San Fran-

cisco, got out of hand when some three hundred thousand fans, far more than anyone had expected, showed up. The event quickly turned into a nightmare of drug casualties, overflowing toilets, faulty sound systems, and brutal violence.

Much of the violence stemmed from the Hell's Angels motorcycle gang, hired as security for five hundred dollars worth of beer. The Stones had expected bikers like the relatively nonviolent British Angels; instead they got a gang wielding knives and weighted pool cues. There were three deaths at Altamont, including that of a young man, Meredith Hunter, who apparently drew a gun while the Stones were onstage and was fatally knifed by Angels.

To some the disaster at Altamont signalled the end of the sixties. It is true that the counterculture, so promising only a few years before, was waning. Psychedelia was proving to be a short-lived fad. The drug- and alcohol-related deaths of three prominent rockers—Janis Joplin, Jimi

The largest and most famous of the rock festivals took place over three days in the summer of 1969 in the small town of Bethel, NY. The crowd was so large that Bethel, for three days, was the third-largest city in the state of New York.

Hendrix, and Jim Morrison—added to the feeling that the era was ending. Furthermore, the messy breakup of the biggest rock group of them all, the Beatles, took place during late 1969 and early 1970, breaking the hearts of fans the world over.

While the sixties held sway, rock had blossomed into many diverse styles. Artists became increasingly free to create exactly what they wanted, and studios developed the sophisticated technical abilities to help them.

Just as importantly, within the space of a few years rock had become an indelible part of life. It was no longer outsider culture or force-fed commercial product; it was, without a doubt, the dominant form of pop music. Geoffrey Stokes writes:

> In political terms, rock had won a landslide as great as Lyndon Johnson's in 1964 or Ronald Reagan's twenty years later. And as the political analogy suggests, what happened next was inevitable. As the aftermath of those elections demonstrates, when you win by too much, your coalition breaks up.[71]

As Stokes suggests, in the next years rock splintered into ever-more-divided segments.

7 The Early Seventies

The most valuable lesson learned by rockers over the course of the 1970s was how to be professional without turning into hacks.

— critic Ken Tucker

It's amazing how far you can get in this business just by showing up for your appointments on time.

— Peter Buck of REM

Fake the funk and your nose will grow.

— George Clinton of
Parliament/Funkadelic

In the fifties rock and roll served a single generation of teenagers, but a far larger audience was brought in by the Beatles and other stars of the sixties. Older rock fans wanted to hear the sounds they had grown up with, but the younger generation demanded something different. Few self-respecting rock fans ever dig what their parents dug.

As audiences in the seventies grew increasingly divided by age, class, race, education, and gender, the music scene fragmented. Trends in the presentation of music reflected these larger audiences, with

elaborately staged concerts in larger arenas. Meanwhile, the music industry expanded into a multibillion-dollar army of record company executives, radio station heads, managers, promoters, and musicians.

This dramatic growth led to changes in the structure of the music industry. Many record executives from the early days of rock were being replaced by lawyers and accountants more concerned with profits than with interesting music. Also, giant international companies, often with little feel for the music, began to buy out smaller companies. For instance, several significant record companies, including Warner Brothers, Reprise, Elektra, Asylum, and Atlantic, were assimilated into one entity by a parent company that had gotten its start with funeral homes and parking lots.

By 1973 six giant corporations controlled nearly 70 percent of the top one hundred singles and albums. Musicians who treasured independence and creativity felt the pressure. Keith Richards comments that at one time

> rock & roll was just peanuts to the money people, and therefore you could take chances, because they didn't really give a damn. But now, the price tag on puttin' out an album, and the video and the stage show—there's

so much investment in it that everybody's playin' safe.[72]

Big Stars

Another aspect of this emphasis on profit, in the wake of the Beatles' breakup, was a frantic hunt for the next big thing, the next Beatles. No one reached that mythic high point, although several artists—often dubbed "stadium acts" to reflect the venues they performed in—did become wildly successful.

They typically did this by appealing to many audiences; that is, like the Beatles, they had something for everyone. They could play both soft ballads and hard rock in styles that typically were glossy, polished, and technically perfect. Critics rightly complained that these attributes were often achieved at the cost of warmth and personal touch. Some groups, such as cult favorites Steely Dan, successfully com-bined polished studio technique with complex, soulful music; more often than not during the seventies, however, the passion of rock was filtered out.

Emblematic of the decade's stadium rock was Fleetwood Mac, which had evolved from a London blues band to glossy Los Angeles pop-rockers. With the addition of Americans Lindsay Buckingham and Stevie Nicks, the band hit gold and their 1975 self-titled LP and 1977's *Rumours* became two of the best-selling albums in history. Sandpaper-voiced Rod Stewart also rose from obscure roots, finding fame with albums that combined folk and R&B with Stewart's own boozy, good-natured writing style; 1971's *Every Picture Tells a Story* and a single from it, "Maggie May," marked the first time a song or an album topped both the U.S. and British charts simultaneously.

Elton John's bravura stage act, unlike the dangerously out-of-control stage personas of someone like Jerry Lee Lewis, was over-the-top in a cheerfully calculated way;

Elton John used over-the-top costumes and stage shows to transform himself from ordinary-looking piano player into a glossy rock star.

John used huge glasses, ridiculous hats, platform shoes, and other silly props to transform himself—a balding, chubby piano player—into a glittering rock star. But John's real gift was for melodies and hooks that lodged in listeners' heads; his grasp of how to craft a good pop song was evident from his first hit, "Your Song," in 1970.

Like most of his hit singles throughout the decade, "Your Song" was written with lyricist Bernie Taupin. Taupin claimed he spent about an hour on each song and was proud of the throwaway nature of his work:

> A lot of times it's good to write disposable songs . . . . They're in the charts, and three months later they're just completely forgotten and nobody bothers with them again. I think that's healthy in a way. You should always have fresh material coming along.[73]

Chirper-Cleffers

Some of the decade's most personal music came from the burgeoning singer-songwriter genre, an extension of the folk-rock of the sixties. The term *singer-songwriter* was a catchall phrase, generally referring to musicians who concentrated on writing and interpreting their own songs. Accompaniment tended to be sparse and quiet, and the songwriting tended toward the introspective and self-absorbed. The industry journal *Variety*, using its trademark wordplay, sometimes irreverently referred to these ever-sensitive performers as "chirper-cleffers."

Some performers were seasoned folk-rockers, such as Paul Simon of Simon and Garfunkel. Others were holdovers from even earlier days; Carole King, a veteran of the Brill Building, spectacularly revitalized her career with 1971's *Tapestry*, which sold more than 10 million copies and remains a milestone in the singer-songwriter genre. Others who emerged in the seventies ranged from the playful (Cat Stevens) to the dark (Leonard Cohen), from the droll (Randy Newman) to the ardent (Jackson Browne), from the eccentric (Tom Waits) to the soulful (Laura Nyro).

Perhaps most representative of the style were James Taylor and Joni Mitchell, both of whom have influenced and inspired dozens of others. Journalist Patrick MacDonald asserts that "Joni Mitchell . . . is the mother of almost every female singer working today, from Alanis Morrissette to Sarah McLachlan to Stevie Nicks."[74]

Taylor and Mitchell set the standard for sensitive, intensely introspective writing that focused on themselves. Others preferred to create separate characters and tell stories through these other voices. Singer-songwriter Randy Newman remarks, "I don't interest me, writing about me . . . . There's a whole world of people and there's no reason why a songwriter should be limited anymore than a short story writer or a novelist."[75]

Headbanger's Ball

Singer-songwriters carefully maintained an aura of intimacy and politeness with audiences. At the other end of the spectrum, however, was another emerging branch of rock. Heavy metal's headbanging attitude took the opposite tack. Since subtle gestures were lost on huge arena crowds, metal was deliberately overdramatic.

Providing the Soundtrack

David Lee Roth, the ebullient singer who rose to fame with Van Halen, comments here on why he thinks heavy metal has been such an enduring style. This excerpt is from an interview in Mikal Gilmore's Night Beat.

"I don't speak for kids, and I don't represent people. I'm simply one of the people. But I'll tell you this much: When that crowd out there tonight went nuts, they weren't going nuts because David Lee Roth is so cool, or because Van Halen is so hot. They went nuts because they were enjoying *themselves.*

That's what we mean when we say there's a little Van Halen in all of us and we're just trying to bring it out. It's like something bursts inside of you, something that makes you not care what people around you are thinking. It makes you feel invincible—like, if a car hit you, nothin' would happen. It should make you feel like the Charge of the Light Brigade, even if you're just going to the bathroom. When you do that on a mass level, it becomes hysterical, not political. It expands to a large group of people not caring about conventions, just getting into the thrill of being themselves. That experience is about the audience, not us. All we do is provide the soundtrack."

Bands used volume and effects like lighting and fireworks that reached even the farthest reaches of a stadium.

The term *heavy metal*, coined by Beat-era writer William Burroughs, was first used in a musical context in Steppenwolf's 1968 hit "Born to Be Wild." Critic Lester Bangs later applied it to an emerging musical style that disdained more genteel rock. Stylistically, metal had roots in such early experiments in guitar distortion as Link Wray's "Rumble" (1958) and Jimi Hendrix. The British Invasion also contributed when one of its premier guitarists, Jimmy Page,

founded Led Zeppelin, the prototype for virtually all future metal. Meanwhile, Dave Davies, the Kinks' guitarist, has long claimed credit for the style, boasting, "It wasn't called heavy metal when I invented it."[76]

Among the most prominent seventies metal bands, those which perfected the genre's classic combination of screaming guitar, histrionic vocals, and crashing rhythm section, were Deep Purple, Kiss, Bachman-Turner Overdrive, T. Rex, Blue Oyster Cult, and Grand Funk Railroad. For many fans, however, the quintessential group was Led Zeppelin.

*Heavy metal pioneers
Led Zeppelin.*

Led Zeppelin stood apart for its blend of several elements: guitarist Jimmy Page's blazing, virtuosic guitar solos; the mesmerizing beat of the rhythm section; and a deep interest in the blues, mysticism, and Celtic mythology shared by Page and singer Robert Plant. These elements combined to produce recordings like "Stairway to Heaven," which begins as a quiet folkie tune, ends in full-bore metal mode, and is reportedly the most-requested song of all time on FM radio. Live, the band was even more powerful. As rock critic Timothy White writes, "The spell they cast was a potent one. Few groups could control a vast crowd with the broody confidence of Led Zeppelin."[77]

Some seventies musicians sought to combine rock with the pomp of classical music in a style called art rock or progressive rock.

The most prominent art rockers were British. The Moody Blues are considered by many to be the first, for their 1966 rock-orchestra recording *Days of Future Passed.* Electric Light Orchestra merged a Beatlesque sound with a similar orchestral approach. Yes and Emerson, Lake, and Palmer brought the art-pomp movement to a climax, mixing rock and classical styles with elements of elaborate fantasy. Bands like Tangerine Dream, meanwhile, concentrated on the hazy, trance-music textures made possible through the use of rapidly developing synthesizers.

Some critics and fans consider the so-called rock opera to be a spin-off of the classical-rock movement. However, many works that are considered rock operas use little in the way of genuine classical influences; they might be more accurately called rock song cycles, since they are series of songs strung together to form a story.

The first rock opera was probably "A Quick One While He's Away," created by Pete Townshend for the Who's second album in 1966 when he realized the record was ten minutes short. "A Quick One" was just a warm-up exercise for Townshend; his full-length "rock opera" *Tommy* appeared in 1969. Townshend has always claimed *Tommy* was light entertainment, but many fans and critics took very seriously the slight story about "that deaf, dumb, and blind boy" who becomes a pinball wizard. *Tommy* was enormously popular and spawned many offshoots, including a live staged opera, a movie, and symphonic versions.

No Restrictions or Rules

In "Be Happy! Don't Worry," an essay reprinted in The Penguin Book of Rock and Roll Writing, *Nik Cohn describes the otherworldy aspects of rock-and-roll touring—in this case, with the Who.*

"The first thing is the unreality. On the road you live in a capsule, a time machine, completely insulated against all normality or balance. You exist entirely in interiors—hotels and airports, limousines, dressing-rooms—and everything that you see has been filtered through glass. Night and day become meaningless, and cities are interchangeable. There are no restrictions or rules, and so you pass directly into fiction.

Each day presents a different gig, therefore a different landscape, therefore a different movie. There is no continuity, which means that you can do precisely as you choose, you can sink yourself and wallow in every possible and impossible outrage, excess, invention, since tomorrow you will be in a different script and everything will start afresh. You can't be reached and you can't be tied. Locked up safely inside your capsule, you skim above all retributions; can pretend to be infinite. . . .

That's the benefit; the major drawback is psychosis. In a world without restrictions, there are also no guidelines, nothing left to cling to. You drift in weightlessness and, unless you have real resources of strength and imagination, this drives you into delirium."

LA Country and Southern Rock

A number of country-influenced bands, direct outgrowths of sixties country-rock, flourished in the 1970s.

One branch of seventies country-rock was known as LA country. Its preeminent band, the Eagles, came together to back a gifted country-influenced singer, Linda Ronstadt, on her 1970 album *Silk Purse*. The Eagles mixed a Byrds-style, laid-back country feel with the slick pop sound and jaded worldview associated with southern California.

The band's anthem to mellowness, "Take It Easy," and the debut album from which it came in 1972, were both enormous hits. A steady string of hits, including "Lyin' Eyes" and "Hotel California," sustained them through the 1970s. Though condemned by some for sounding smug and soft, the Eagles were hugely popular thanks to what writer Timothy White calls their "indigenous [original], post-Beach Boys brand of romance."[78]

Southern rock, as its name suggests, was a regional style that mixed traditional country, the churning beat of Texas-style blues, and hard rock into a boisterous, hard-drinking, quick-fisted cocktail. The best-known southern rockers were the Allman Brothers Band, a multiracial group led by slide-guitar virtuoso Duane Allman (a legendary performer who had recorded with soul stars Aretha Franklin and Wilson Pickett) and his singer-keyboardist brother, Gregg.

The band's signature interplay of its twin lead guitars—Allman and Dickie Betts playing off each other in extended jams—became the defining sound of the southern rock style. It has been imitated and enlarged upon by many other good-old-boy southern bands, including the Charlie Daniels Band, the Marshall Tucker Group, .38 Special, and Lynyrd Skynyrd. The Allmans' live album *At Fillmore East* (1971) still stands as a classic of the genre.

Tragically, Duane Allman was killed in a motorcycle crash in Georgia just months after the record's release, and soon after bassist Berry Oakley died in a similar wreck. Though the band persevered without them, it never regained its strong early momentum.

Disco Dis Way, Disco Dat Way

One musical style of the 1970s, disco, had a short but forceful reign over musical trends.

Disco's roots were in black clubs of the 1950s, with their tradition of dancing to records instead of live bands. In the 1960s a European fad for discotheques, as they were called in French, briefly swept America; celebrities like Jackie Kennedy and Liz Taylor performed the latest dance steps at fashionable clubs like the Peppermint Lounge.

In the early seventies discos reappeared in the gay/Latino/black subcultures of New York as intimate places where these minority groups could relax and be themselves. Discos were for dancing, and their true stars were the disc jockeys, whose job was to find the hottest records and provide the soundtrack for nonstop movement.

Musically, disco was simple enough. Its basis was a relentless, poundingly loud rhythm that emphasized every beat. Anything could then be laid on top of the beat: Mozart melodies, wiggly synthesizer figures, screaming psychedelic guitar, or ecstatic gospel vocals.

As the music spread and entered the pop mainstream, several singers became stars. Among these were American singer Donna Summer and her German producer Giorgio Moroder, deep-voiced Barry White, the Swedish quartet Abba, and the Village People, a cartoonish group parodying gay stereotypes. Dozens of others had disco hits as well, many of them one-shot wonders, and a number of established artists, including Rod Stewart, the Beach Boys, and the Rolling Stones, also dabbled in disco.

Perhaps the most successful of all were the Bee Gees, three Australian brothers who scored massively when *Saturday Night Fever*, a 1977 film for which they supplied some of the music, became a monster hit. The soundtrack album sold 30 million copies, and John Travolta's electrifying performance in the movie as a white-suited dance king became an instantly recognized (and much parodied) symbol of the disco culture.

Disco's excesses inspired a strong backlash among hard-rockers, including public burnings of disco records by disgruntled DJs. Meanwhile, the disco lifestyle, with its emphasis on (often hollow) elegance and sophistication, began to fade after a few

Like a City Street

Critic Tom Smucker, in this excerpt from The Rolling Stone History of Rock and Roll, *summarizes the dual nature of disco, its intimacy as well as its complete anonymity.*

"At its best, disco wasn't really much like a big private club, and certainly not like a family, a commune, a tribe, or a world view. It was like a city street. A place where strangers could interact with one another if they wanted to without having to become like one another. It reminded us that cities aren't just places where people get mugged. If the vibes are right, they're places where people can be stimulated, lots of happy accidents can happen, and even strangers can fall in love."

Disco boogied its way into American dance clubs in the 1970s.

In the early 1970s singers like Marvin Gaye began to address complex, and often disturbing, political realities in their music.

years, succeeded by hip-hop and other forms of black dance music. In its day, however, disco was a potent force. If nothing else, it provoked strong reactions. Critic Mikal Gilmore writes that disco was both "one of the most popular and reviled [hated] mileposts in pop music's history."[79]

What's Goin' On?

Disco was determinedly nonpolitical; it cared about little but boogying. Other forms of black music in the seventies, however, were restless, political, and hard-edged.

Sly Stone continued to deeply influence other musicians, especially with his controversial 1971 album *There's A Riot Goin' On.* It combined brilliantly dark, disjointed music with lyrics about violence, drug abuse, and armed revolution. Compared with the explicitness of some of today's music, the album seems relatively tame, but at the time it caused a furor. Unfortunately, Stone's personal troubles, including increasingly erratic behavior and a serious drug problem, kept him from reaching his potential.

Other black musicians were also creating confrontational music. Motown had always carefully avoided any kind of controversy, and its chief, Berry Gordy, at first refused to let Marvin Gaye release his highly political album *What's Goin' On.* The singer insisted, and the album touched a deep nerve with the public, becoming one of the label's biggest sellers. As rock historian Robert Palmer writes, "Like James Brown, [Motown producer] Norman Whitfield, Sly Stone, and Stevie Wonder, Marvin Gaye saw 'pushing the envelope' as both a privilege and a duty: This was what being an artist was all about."[80]

Gaye's success with the album, and with renegotiating his contract to give him greater artistic and financial freedom, helped spur another of Motown's most talented performers. Stevie Wonder had been a star since the age of ten, but Motown had kept him on a tight leash. The company had controlled his publishing and musical arrangements, overseen his production, booked his tours, and held his money in trust. It is estimated that Wonder earned over $30 million by 1970 but received only $1 million.

Wonder's own discussions with Motown about his contract and recording privileges began in 1971, when the singer turned twenty-one, and ended in 1975, when he signed a multimillion-dollar contract that also gave him unprecedented artistic control. The resulting midseventies albums (including *Music of My Mind, Talking Book,* and *Innervisions*) combined Wonder's studio brilliance with a concern about social and spiritual issues, and they sealed his reputation as one of the most innovative black musicians of the decade.

Make It Funky

Some black musicians of the era maintained classic traditions, such as the sublime Al Green (the heart of Memphis soul in the seventies) or Gamble and Huff (the masterminds behind the Philly Sound brand of dance music). Many observers, however, feel that the most important black music to emerge from the seventies was funk.

Disco seemed to exist only in the moment, but funk was conscious of its musical roots. In particular, it borrowed heavily from the innovations of the sixties, particularly those sounds—"choked" guitars, clipped rhythms, staccato horns, and heavy bass—pioneered by James Brown and Sly Stone. Rock critic Ken Tucker writes, "Disco wanted you to think that [it] had been invented yesterday [but funk] wanted you to know it had a past."[81]

A number of bands experimented with funk, including the Watts Band; Kool and the Gang; the Ohio Players; and Earth, Wind, and Fire. Many observers feel that its highest form was produced by one wild group: the extended family of musicians that appeared under the umbrella of Parliament/Funkadelic (P-Funk).

Parliament and its sister band, Funkadelic, were led by George Clinton, a visionary who mixed elements of traditional black R&B with a wildly eclectic range of influences. A P-Funk song could contain everything from a slashing Hendrix guitar to complex polyrhythms, jazzy horns, old-fashioned harmony vocals, space-age electronics, and heavy metal. The band's irrepressible stage shows, meanwhile, featured bizarre costumes and complex stage effects, such as a giant "mothership" that brought the cosmic musicians into the hall.

Mixed in with this was Clinton's extravagant, cartoonish philosophy, which freely mixed racial pride with science fiction, sexual liberation, cosmic mythology, and more. No matter what direction the band went in, however, it was always accessible and always funky. Rock critic Joe McEwen writes that the "mixture of tribal funk, elaborate stage props and the relentless assault on personal inhibition resembled nothing so much as a Space Age Mardi Gras."[82]

By the middle of the decade many musicians and fans were beginning to tire of styles like funk, heavy metal, singer-songwriters, disco, and stadium rock. A strong backlash was developing against what was seen as music's excessiveness, monotony, and blandness. In 1976 a new idiom directly attacked this flabbiness. It was called punk.

8 New Energy from the Underground

We were all really disgusted with what was going on in rock and roll. . . . There was no excitement in the music anymore, no fun or color or character or personality.

— Joey Ramone of the Ramones

Rock (and many of its offshoots, such as psychedelia and disco) had once been an underground movement; now it was an accepted part of the mainstream music culture. But its increasing commercialism had made it slack and flabby, and radio's tight programming further curbed creativity. What is more, rock's enormous profits had distanced stars from their fans; musicians had once been more or less the same kind of people as their audiences, but now they were pampered celebrities.

Rock's needed shot in the arm came from a new underground movement, punk music, along with its close cousin, new wave, and reggae, a musical style from Jamaica that became closely associated with punk.

The punk revolution of 1976 was a direct reaction to the complacency and cynicism of the mainstream rock industry. One rock celebrity, Rod Stewart, was often singled out as the supreme symbol of bloated, decadent rock stardom. Stewart had once been a talented bad boy of music; now, his detractors charged, he had surrendered his talent to crass commercial interests.

In response to the boring music they heard in the mainstream, punks questioned everything that the established musical culture assumed, from basic ideas of melody and harmony to ideals of pristine studio sound and music as a form of community. By throwing those assumptions out the window, punk returned rock to its raw, basic roots.

Underground musical movements may be wildly different, but they usually have one characteristic in common. All are grassroots movements, started not by established professionals but by rank outsiders. Critic Ken Tucker notes that punk and its related styles were "would-be popular musics created by the same kinds of people who had invented rock and roll—the disenfranchised, the visionary, the eccentric, the despised but ambitious."[83]

Punk's Predecessors

Arrogant rebellion by outsiders has always been a major element of rock. In the fifties it was Elvis, Little Richard, and Jerry

Lee Lewis; in the sixties it was Mick Jagger, Jimi Hendrix, and hundreds of anonymous, amateur garage bands formed by enthusiastic teens in the wake of the British Invasion.

These protopunk bands, not surprisingly called garage bands since that's where most of them played, mixed surf instrumentals and R&B with Invasion-style pop and whatever else they could find. The result was crude, but it did the trick. According to critic Robot A. Hull, "Garage rock was, in essence, teenage desire directly translated into twanging and pounding and thump-thumping [as an] adolescent need to make noise and to create disharmony wherever possible."[84]

Most of these bands stayed in the garage. A handful made a record or two, and some of these went national: Sam the Sham and the Pharoahs' "Wooly Bully," ? and the Mysterians' "96 Tears," The Seeds' "Pushin' Too Hard," and the ultimate garage classic, the Kingsmen's "Louie Louie."

A few, meanwhile, became seriously influential. One was the Stooges, whose singer, Iggy Stooge (later Iggy Pop), became infamous for rolling onstage bare-chested amidst broken glass and hurling himself heedlessly into the audience. Most influential of all, however, was New York's Velvet Underground.

Led by a Welsh-born, classically trained viola player, John Cale, and a New York songwriter-guitarist-singer, Lou Reed, the band was taken under the wing of pop artist Andy Warhol in 1965. Warhol used the band as part of his "Exploding Plastic Inevitable," an experimental series of mixed-media "happenings." The artist also designed the famous peelable-banana cover of Velvet Underground's first album.

Instead of typical garage songs about parties and mindless fun, Reed's songs confronted such subjects as rough sex, drugs, and violent street life. Though the Velvets never sold many records, their uncompromising music set the stage for future punk.

"That Spark"

Lenny Kaye, guitarist of the Patti Smith Group, comments in Robert Palmer's Rock and Roll: An Unruly History *on the contrast between mainstream seventies rock and garage bands.*

"Garage bands became more important in the early seventies because rock and roll had gotten very complicated. Progressive rock was an adult medium; instrumental prowess and musicianship were the driving force. Even though I like a lot of that stuff, something was lacking: the fact that you could learn to play three chords and get up onstage within a week. That spark, that desire, that's the kind of thing that makes rock and roll tick. I think that's why it began in the first place: It's a music for the person who needs to make music."

Rock critic David Fricke writes, "Just about every punk, post-punk and avant-pop artist or band of the past two decades owes a debt of inspiration, if not direct influence, to the Velvet Underground."[85]

"Beat on the Brat"

Punk took shape nearly simultaneously in two cities that had always been magnets for musical innovators: London and New York. Though other cities fostered strong punk scenes (Los Angeles, for instance, with the Germs, Black Flag, the Circle Jerks, X, and Fear), London and New York were the important centers.

American punk bands heavily influenced English punk, and vice versa; though there is evidence that the New York scene developed first, the two were so close in time that they can be considered nearly concurrent.

New York punk first emerged around 1974 with a handful of bands that appeared regularly at two clubs, Max's Kansas City and CBGB. The New York Dolls were a raunchy hard-rock outfit, much given to glittery costumes. The Patti Smith Group and Television were more influenced by intellectuals such as the French poets Paul Verlaine and Arthur Rimbaud, and their music was convoluted, opaque, and arty. One Max's/CBGB band, however, is often singled out as the first and foremost American punk band.

The Ramones wore what amounted to a band uniform: torn jeans, ratty sneakers, ripped T-shirts, and black leather jackets. Their songs were ultrafast, ultraloud joyrides with no solos and goofy, deliberately nonintellectual titles like "Beat on the Brat" and "Now I Wanna Sniff Some Glue." Each Ramones song sounded just like the one before it, counted off with glee by bassist Dee Dee Ramone. Guitarist Johnny Ramone explains wryly, "It just came natural to him; he counted to four really well."[86]

This cartoonish band, which might seem like no more than a novelty act, was met with a mixture of awe and ridicule. But behind their friendly moron fronts, the Ramones were hard workers, and this strong work ethic took their music outside the closed world of downtown Manhattan clubs to the world outside.

The first Ramones record (fourteen songs in under thirty minutes, produced for six thousand dollars) and the band's appearances in England in 1976 were the main inspiration for the full-fledged punk revolution that took hold in London that year. Longtime rock critic Kurt Loder sums up the band's impact on mainstream seventies rock when he writes, "The Ramones . . . landed in this flabbed-out scene like a boulder on a box of sugar-cream doughnuts. Their debut album . . . was perhaps the purest expression of head-first rock velocity in the music's history."[87]

No Future

One difference between New York punk bands and their London equivalents was that American bands like the Ramones were more conscious of their garage-band predecessors. Journalist Caroline Coon noted in 1976 that British musicians deliberately turned their back on previous influences: "The British punk scene . . . is disgusted by the past. Nostalgia is a dirty word."[88]

Early British punk bands like the Damned experimented with raw and often violent music that stripped rock to its bare bones—blasting guitar chords, massive bass, frantic rhythm, and screaming vocals. Their clothing, meanwhile, was a fashion of no-fashion: ripped T-shirts, torn jeans or leather bondage pants, frayed leather jackets, and worn sneakers. Hair was severely cropped or worn in provocative, multi-hued cuts.

London punk was also far more political than its American counterpart. Specifically, it railed against the conservative politics of Prime Minister Margaret Thatcher. Her economic and social programs angered and frustrated many young people, especially those from working-class backgrounds. They saw no future for themselves in a social climate that witnessed such problems as high unemployment, poor wages, and frequent violence between racist skinheads and immigrants, not to mention a boring music scene.

In the seedy halls of the early punk scene, audiences and musicians goaded each other with anything at hand, including flying bodies, beer cans, or spit. The dance floor was a mass of writhing bodies bashing into one another in an airborne dance called the pogo, so named for its resemblance to a roomful of sweaty human pogo sticks.

Often the bands could barely play their instruments, in keeping with one basic aspect of early rock and roll: the spirit of democracy, in which anyone and everyone could be a musician. For punks, the ability to play an instrument was, according to music journalist John Tobler, "a poor second to enthusiasm and attitude."[89]

Ground zero for London punks was a clothing boutique known variously as Let It Rock, Too Fast to Live, Too Young to Die, and Sex. Its colorful owner, Malcolm McLaren, promoted a style that included spiked hair, heavy boots, and clothing that was disassembled and pinned back together.

McLaren was also an aspiring music promoter, and he masterminded the formation of a band from some of his customers. The Sex Pistols, as the band was eventually named, was so short-lived that it put out only one studio album, but it was one of the most important bands in rock. As rock journalist Al Spicer points out, "Now and again, a band comes along and takes a sledgehammer to the definition of rock music. The Sex Pistols were one of those bands."[90]

"Working with What You Got"

In his oral history of punk Please Kill Me, *Legs McNeil summarizes the movement's ideals.*

"The music was really about corrupting every form—it was about advocating kids to not wait to be told what to do, but make life up for themselves, it was about trying to get people to use their imaginations again, it was about not being perfect, it was about saying it was okay to be amateurish and funny, that real creativity came out of making a mess, it was about working with what you got in front of you and turning everything embarrassing, awful, and stupid in your life to your advantage."

By the end of the 1970s mainstream rock was getting too watered down for some tastes. This disenchantment with rock's establishment created a ripe atmosphere for the rise of punk bands like the Ramones.

Here's the Sex Pistols

Looking to assemble a band that could combine working-class rage with his own intellectual ideas about art and anarchy, McLaren chose young men with minimal musical skills but maximum shock value. Referring to a completely fabricated group that starred in a midsixties television show, critic Ken Tucker writes, "In one sense, the Pistols were as manufactured a rock band as the Monkees had been."[91]

In addition to guitarist Steve Jones, bassist Glen Matlock, and drummer Paul Cook, the Pistols included a snarling dervish of a singer, Johnny Rotten. According to legend, his name came from the state of his dental work, and he endeared himself to McLaren by wearing a shirt with the Pink Floyd logo, above which he had scrawled "I HATE." Although Rotten barely had a singing voice, he was, nonetheless, an original, not someone who copied his style from American singers. According to his near-contemporary Elvis Costello, "He was the first actual English rock & roll singer."[92]

The group's first appearance—at an art school in November 1975—ended after ten minutes when the school's social programmer unplugged their amps. Though ignored by the press and music industry, they persevered and emerged as the top punk band within months. When word of mouth about them could no longer be ignored, the EMI label released the group's first single, "Anarchy in the U.K.," at the end of 1976.

Even though the single shot onto the British charts, EMI dropped the band due to a controversy (the host of a televised interview goaded the Pistols into uttering

The Punk scene developed in two cities simultaneously, London and New York. Singer Johnny Rotten fronted the legendary London punk group called the Sex Pistols.

obscenities) and withdrew the single. Matlock then left, reportedly under pressure because he was too fond of melodic music. He was replaced by Sid Vicious, who couldn't play but had the appropriate attitude.

The band was signed to an American label, then dropped a week later. The label refused to release the band's second single, "God Save the Queen." It was eventually released on another label and immediately banned from airplay by the government-run British Broadcasting Corporation, as an offense to the monarchy. It became a top seller anyway, with its space on published chart lists marked by a blank.

Essentially barred from England—no hall would book them—the Pistols toured Europe and America, inspiring miniriots in several cities. When their album *Never Mind the Bollocks Here's the Sex Pistols* was released, several major British stores refused to stock it; nonetheless, the record went to number one. As Kurt Loder writes,

> Nothing in rock was ever quite the same after *Never Mind the Bollocks*. The Sex Pistols swept away the cozy corporate musical verities [accepted truths] of the seventies in a tidal wave of spit and derision . . . [plus] a profound contempt for all things phony and overinflated in the established culture.[93]

London Calling

Always shaky, the band's cohesiveness became more precarious in America. By the end of the tour, Jones and Cook were not speaking to the others, and everyone was hostile toward what they saw as McLaren's crass attempt to cash in on notoriety. Vicious had developed a serious heroin habit, and he was such a poor musician that his amp was turned off when the band played. (Soon after the end of the tour,

Still Punk

In Mikal Gilmore's Night Beat, *bassist Paul Simenon of the Clash summarizes his philosophy of punk.*

"You know, people ask me all the time if we're still punk, and I always say, 'Yeah, we're punk,' because punk meant not having to stick to anybody else's rules. Then you look around and see all these bands that are afraid to break the rules of what they think punk is. We're punk because we still have our own version of what it means. That's what it is: an attitude. And we'll stay punk as long as we can keep the blindfolds off."

The longest-lasting and most influential group of the punk era was the London-based band called the Clash.

while out on bail after his arrest for his girlfriend's murder, Vicious died of an overdose. He was twenty-one years old.)

At the end of the show, at the tour's final stop in San Francisco in January 1978, just before his public announcement that he was quitting the band, Rotten asked the crowd, "Ever have the feeling you've been cheated?"[94] Many assumed the comment had been directed at the audience. However, he commented later that it had been aimed elsewhere: "That wasn't directed at the audience. It was directed at us onstage, because we had been cheated, and we cheated ourselves."[95]

The Pistols left a strong legacy, inspiring dozens of bands. Though most of these never achieved more than a brief popularity, some survived, including the Damned (whose single "New Rose" was released a few weeks before the Pistols's debut), the Buzzcocks, X-Ray Spex, the Jam, the Au Pairs, the Mekons, the Gang of Four, and Siouxsie and the Banshees.

The longest-lasting and most influential of these was the Clash. They had both power and versatility, as shown in their seminal work, *London Calling*, an ambitious double album mixing punkish energy with rockabilly, reggae, and R&B. "When the Pistols disbanded in early 1978," writes critic Mikal Gilmore, "the rock press and punks alike [regarded] the Clash as the movement's central symbol and hope."[96]

New Wave

The term *new wave* loosely covers a strain of music that used elements of both punk and pop. New wave bands, sometimes called power pop bands, tended to be more commercially oriented, with styles that fit relatively easily into radio formats.

Though some prominent American new wave bands emerged from smaller cities (notably Pere Ubu of Cleveland and REM and the B-52s of Athens, Georgia), most American new wavers came from urban centers. Boston produced the quirky Jonathan Richman and the Modern Lovers as well as the Cars, whose catchy, radio-friendly tunes were rooted in Ric Ocasek's cool delivery.

In New York, Blondie and Talking Heads were part of of the punkish CBGB/Max's Kansas City scenes. Blondie was built around the icy charisma of its lead singer, Debbie Harry. David Byrne, Talking Heads' leader, merged a love of black funk and world music with his own eye-popping, eccentric stage presence, connecting with avant-garde British producer Brian Eno to make music that was both adventurous and commercially successful.

Two groups bridged the American and British new wave movements. American Chrissie Hynde worked with various bands (including early versions of the Clash and the Damned) before forming the Pretenders in London with three Englishmen. The band stood out thanks to its ringing guitar sound, Hynde's throaty, vibrato-filled voice, and her anthemic, tough-girl songs.

Another prominent Anglo-American new wave group was the Police. The band's appeal lay in its spare instrumentation (using only a guitar, bass, and drums), the influence of reggae, their distinctive blond looks (originally created for a chewing-gum commercial), and the brilliantly catchy, highly commercial songs of Sting, the band's bassist and singer.

Elvis C.

A branch of British music associated with new wave was pub rock, a cheerful mix of R&B and old-fashioned rock and roll that was the opposite of punk's dark nihilism. Many prominent pub rock bands recorded for an independent label, Stiff Records, whose coowner, Nick Lowe, played a pivotal role in British new wave, producing many of the era's classic records and forging his own career as a singer and songwriter.

Among Lowe's productions was the first album by a gifted musician who helped extend 1970s singer-songwriter traditions into the next era: Elvis Costello. (Costello's real name is Declan McManus; he took his stage name as a joke, but after "the real" Elvis's

New wave performers like Elvis Costello picked up where the singer-songwriters of the early seventies left off.

death in 1977 the joke soured. Costello seriously considered renaming himself but did not do so in the end.)

Costello captured immediate attention from both critics and fans with his deadpan wordplay, bitter humor, multiple layers of irony, and fierce intelligence. The Lowe-produced *My Aim Is True* was met with ecstatic praise by critics and fans alike, although the music industry generally snubbed him.

The 1977 Grammy Award for best new artist, for instance, went not to Costello, who many felt clearly deserved it, but to the now-forgotten band A Taste of Honey. The following year, when England's Capitol Radio gave Elton John an award for best male singer of the year, John noted in his acceptance speech that it should have gone to someone else: "Elvis Costello was the most important—by far the best songwriter and the best record-maker."[97]

Rastaman Vibration

A related style that emerged during the punk–new wave years came not from England or America but from an island in the Caribbean.

Reggae, a style of pop music that had thrived in dance halls in Jamaica for years, was characterized by an infectious, hypnotic rhythm and syncopated guitar riffs. Closely associated with the Rastafarian religion, whose followers use marijuana as part of their religious practices, reggae had an influence far beyond its commercial success. Though it never reached a massive audience in America, reggae was a major influence on British bands like the Clash, UB40, and the Police, and it made a handful of Jamaican musicians into stars.

Many Americans were first exposed to reggae in 1972 through three works: a Jamaican movie, *The Harder They Come*; a hit single with a reggae beat, Johnny Nash's "I Can See Clearly Now"; and *Catch a Fire*, the first album by Bob Marley and the Wailers released outside Jamaica.

Marley had long been one of Jamaica's most popular musicians, and in time he would become reggae's ambassador to the world. Marley's success gave the careers of other Jamaican artists a boost. Among these were Burning Spear; Toots and the Maytals, whose lead singer, Toots Hibbert, was strongly affected by American soul; and Peter Tosh, an ex-bandmate of Marley's.

Reggae found a ready audience with punks, a phenomenon celebrated in Marley's song "Punky Reggae Party." In keeping with the highly political nature of both schools, musicians from reggae and punk camps were also linked through their involvement in the music community's anti-racist activities, and in organizations such as the British group Rock Against Racism.

Jamaican singer-songwriter Bob Marley brought the catchy sounds of reggae to a worldwide audience.

Do-It-Yourself

Punks, postpunks, and new wavers in America and England were not always content to just make music. One of the most important legacies of the punk era was the success of independent, do-it-yourself record labels.

In an attempt to circumvent the restrictions of the major record companies, small labels with names like Rough Trade, Rabid, Raw, and Rad Edge sprang up on both sides of the Atlantic. Records from these companies often relied on shows and independent record shops for sales since many were too brutal or obscene for the radio.

One of the most respected independents was SST Records, formed in Los Angeles by guitarist Greg Ginn. SST fostered a stable of bands that formed the core of American postpunk, including Ginn's group, Black Flag, and the Minutemen, Hüsker Dü, and Sonic Youth. Another extremely successful label from southern California was Epitaph, founded by members of the band Bad Religion.

Punk and its related movements blasted the music scene apart in 1976. Well into the 1980s, the impact continued to be felt, even as new styles emerged and new stars ascended.

9 The Eighties and Nineties

Music saved me. From the beginning, my guitar was something I could go to. If I hadn't found music, I don't know what I would have done.

—Bruce Springsteen

Periodically, many people have predicted the death of rock, from the parents and authority figures who thought rock and roll was a quick fad to Johnny Rotten, who boasted, "The Pistols finished rock and roll; they were the last rock and roll band."[98]

As the seventies became the eighties, the music industry fell on hard times, and many observers thought rock had again run its course. These speculations were prompted by serious drops in record sales and concert attendance.

Various theories were advanced to explain the drop-off. Some suggested that the rising popularity of video games was taking away from music. Others pointed to the bland nature of mainstream "corporate" rock, evident as the energy of punk began to wane, and said that audiences were simply bored. Still others felt that inflated prices for albums and concert tickets were to blame.

Instead, the industry recovered with unexpected energy and emerged stronger than ever, revitalized in large part by innovations in technology.

High-Tech

One technological boost was a breakthrough in portable cassette players. Although the Walkman and similar portable devices are commonplace now, when they were introduced to America in 1980 they represented a thrilling, almost revolutionary new way to hear music. Prerecorded tapes experienced a huge surge in sales; by 1983 half of the year's $3.78 billion in recorded-music profits were from cassettes. A year later, cassettes edged past vinyl records in profits.

Then came the compact disc, introduced in the mid-1980s. CDs recorded music as digital signals rather than the cruder analog form of vinyl records. Critics complain that digitized sound is colder and thinner than analog sound, that is, vinyl. Nonetheless, the convenience, durability, and extended length of CDs proved extremely popular, creating a huge new market and pushing CDs to the forefront. Record companies boosted profits by reis-

A technological advance, rather than a musical group, brought the music industry out of a severe slump in the mid-1980s. The introduction of personal cassette players and compact discs caused total music industry revenues to triple between 1984 and 1994.

suing old music in CD form; new music became hard to find, then impossible to find, on vinyl.

The music industry bounced back from its slump. Total revenue for CD, cassette, vinyl, and video sales nearly tripled between 1984 and 1994, from $4.37 billion to $12.06 billion. CDs, meanwhile, continued to lead the way: in 1994 nearly twice as many CDs were sold (662 million) as cassettes (345 million).

Enter Music Video

One of the most profound changes in music technology involved the way people were exposed to new music.

For decades radio had been the primary medium for hearing new tunes. In 1981, however, a new form debuted that combined audio with visuals. Music Television (MTV) was both mesmerizing entertainment and a powerful selling tool, and it changed the course of pop music.

Showing musicians on screen was not a new idea. Rockers of the 1950s had often appeared as themselves in movies of the era, and by the late 1960s top bands like the Beatles routinely made short films for broadcast on TV programs.

As video became increasingly sophisticated and inexpensive, even unknown bands without large resources were able to create their own works. Former Monkee Michael Nesmith introduced the first music video show, *Popclips*, in 1980. Later that year the show's parent cable channel, Warner Amex Satellite Entertainment, expanded *Popclips* into MTV.

MTV was built along the lines of a commercial radio station. The cable network's executives targeted their audience; in this case, twelve- to thirty-four-year-olds, primarily white and male. Accordingly, they programmed a daily playlist of short videos based on current songs, with an emphasis on AOR (adult-oriented) hard rock. As on a radio station, these clips were presented by a team of announcers—video jockeys, or VJs.

MTV was a hit from the beginning; by the end of its first year, its VJ hosts were receiving one hundred thousand fan letters a month. It went on to be the fastest-growing network in cable TV history.

MTV Style

MTV's success affected other areas of the industry. Videos not only boosted sales of albums but also became a multimillion-dollar segment of the industry. Record labels began collaborating with MTV to promote acts by providing tour date information and underwriting contests such as "win a weekend with Van Halen." And the distinctive visual style of music video began to seep into other areas of entertainment, notably the movie *Flashdance* and the television series *Miami Vice.*

MTV, naturally enough, preferred to show videos that were visually interesting. The bands with the most striking videos, such as Eurythmics and Men at Work, were featured heavily, and the exposure proved effective: These bands were extremely successful in America despite relatively little radio airplay.

English acts had a twofold advantage in MTV's early days. First, Britain had a more extensive history of music television shows that used prefilmed visuals, dating back to the Beatles. Second, England was the home of the new romantics, a musical trend that was perfect for video.

The new romantics countered the rawness and nihilism of punk with elaborate costumes, theatrical poses, and highly stylized music. Many took inspiration from David Bowie, who had emerged in the seventies as a master of ironic, sexually ambi-

gious, and adventurous stage personas. Summing up the attitude of new-romantic bands like Duran Duran, Culture Club, Human League, and A Flock of Seagulls, critic Kurt Loder writes, "Why be down when you can be up? Why look terminal when you can look terrific?"[99]

Critical

Since its inception MTV has come under heavy criticism. One of the earliest charges was racism; critics complained that black artists received little or no airplay. They pointed out that in the channel's first eighteen months, 750 videos were shown; less than two dozen of these featured black performers or racially mixed bands.

Many other arguments have been leveled against MTV. Critics charge that, besides shortening viewers' attention spans, robbing artists of mystery by overexposing them, and denigrating women by showing them only in sexually and socially submissive roles, MTV downplays musical creativity in favor of looking good. They point to the example of the duo Milli Vanilli, who did not sing a single note themselves on their hugely popular 1989 album and lip-synched throughout their videos. When this was revealed, the scandal resulted in dozens of lawsuits and the cancellation of the group's Grammy Award for best new artist.

MTV's defenders point out that, starting with Chuck Berry and Elvis Presley, rockers have always placed a strong emphasis on visual appeal. They also note that the channel has grown increasingly sophisticated, providing not just videos but news, concerts, cartoons, dramatic shows, and innovative programming like its *Unplugged* series. Some critics worry that MTV will eclipse other forms of entertainment; it will most likely prove, however, to be simply another form of getting the music out. Rock writer Jon Pareles notes, "For all its far-reaching effects, video has just thrown one more giant variable into the marketing, and the cultural clout, available to rockers who are willing to fully exploit it."[100]

Michael and the Material Girl

Ironically, considering the charges of racism leveled against MTV, the singer who perhaps benefited most from it, and who helped define the very medium, was a black man. Commenting on the extended video for Michael Jackson's song "Thriller," rock writer John Swenson notes that it "set standards for music-video production that the rest of the industry is still trying to live up to."[101]

After a long career with his family of performers, the Jacksons, Michael Jackson scored a breakthrough solo album, *Thriller*. It was everywhere in the summer of 1982, spawning six number-one singles and becoming the best-selling album in history: over 45 million sold and counting. Jackson's visual appeal was equally strong, and the videos accompanying *Thriller's* singles put the charismatic Jackson before an enormous audience.

These clips were far more elaborate and professional than anything yet shown on MTV. The lengthy video for "Thriller," for instance, was directed by a noted film director, John Landis, and used a voice-

Michael Jackson took advantage of a new medium, MTV, to push his album Thriller *to record-breaking sales in 1982.*

over by horror-movie legend Vincent Price as well as makeup by Oscar-winning special effects artist Rick Baker.

Thriller's blend of commercial savvy, narrative style, technology, and Jackson's own inventive singing and dancing set a new standard. It further extended Jackson's audience by cannily using guest stars: heavy-metal guitarist Eddie Van Halen for "Beat It" and Paul McCartney in "The Girl Is Mine." Rock historian Paul Friedlander writes that "Jackson's use of video as a promotional tool, his conceptualization of short stories, and his focus on quality . . . helped to solidify [*Thriller*] as one of the defining popular music moments of the eighties."[102]

Jackson was not the only star to benefit from MTV and other forms of promotion. Madonna Louise Veronica Ciccone emerged in the eighties as a media-savvy performer to rival Bob Dylan or Michael Jackson and as the most controversial star since Elvis.

Madonna's early video-and-song packages, such as "Borderline" (which celebrated interracial romance) and "Papa Don't Preach" (with its message about unwed mothers) were bold and sexy, with consistently strong lyrical and musical content. In the years since, Madonna has fashioned for herself a constantly changing, multifaceted persona. She has also become one of the wealthiest of pop stars, having signed a deal with Time Warner (reputed to top $60 million) to release a range of films, albums, and books.

Since she also wields almost complete control over her fortune and creative outlets, Madonna's combination of a sexy persona with a sly intelligence has become a role model for many women who aspire to power. According to rock writer J. D. Considine,

> Madonna changed the rules on almost every level, restructuring the relationship between image and content . . . and reducing to rubble traditional notions of sex and power. It would be hard to imagine a truer definition of star power.[103]

You Go, Girl

Madonna was only the most obvious example of a strong trend in 1980s rock: the increasingly prominent role of women.

Women had always been part of the music, of course. Though a handful had achieved fame as instrumentalists (such as Maureen Tucker, the drummer for the Velvet Underground, and the veteran bluesrock singer and slide guitarist Bonnie Raitt), often they were limited to singing.

Punk, however, blew away many of rock's preconceived notions, including accepted roles for women in music. If anybody could make rock and roll, as the punks asserted, then women's legitimacy was unquestionable. Singing was OK, but playing was better. Rock critic Holly George-Warren comments on the change: "Rock & roll as played by men—aggressive, sexual, loud!—is what looked like the most fun . . . and promised the greatest release."[104]

A number of punk, postpunk, and new wave bands were all-women, such as the Raincoats and the Slits. Patti Smith and Chrissie Hynde also proved that women could be as aggressively macho as any man. Further examples include Annie Lennox of the Eurythmics, Talking Heads bassist Tina Weymouth, and the bizarre figure of portly, braces-wearing Poly Styrene, leader of X-Ray Spex.

Women continued in strong roles as the eighties progressed, including Ann and Nancy Wilson of Heart, the quirky Cyndi Lauper, rapper Queen Latifah, the Go-Gos (the first all-woman rock band to be a major commercial success), and the confrontational Irishwoman Sinead O'Connor, whose astonishing voice was combined with a no-holds-barred political and social aggressiveness. R&B legend Tina Turner's stunning comeback as a solo artist, meanwhile, was even more successful than her earlier career with exhuband Ike.

The Boss

The eighties were breakthrough years for two of the era's most important rock traditionalists. One was the band U2, which emerged out of Ireland's postpunk scene in 1980 with a fiercely earnest, spiritually hopeful, and unfashionably optimistic outlook that was in sharp contrast to punk's bleakness.

The other was a rocker who had been waiting a long time for his chance at a wide, universal audience. Back in 1974 critic Jon Landau had witnessed a stunning show by a promising young musician from New Jersey. "I saw rock & roll's future," Landau raved, "and its name is Bruce Springsteen."[105]

Springsteen was a breath of fresh air in those dull days, offering an alternative to the current menu of tired music. His electrifying live shows and ambitious songwriting promised a return to the vitality and passion of an earlier era. Springsteen's career, however, stalled. Despite massive

---

Maintaining Connections

In this excerpt from an interview in The Rolling Stone Interviews: The 1980s, *Bruce Springsteen muses on the difficulty of fame.*

"One of the things that was always on my mind to do was to maintain connections with the people I'd grown up with, and the sense of the community where I came from. . . . The danger of fame is in forgetting, or being distracted. You see it happen to so many people. Elvis's case must have been tremendously difficult. . . . The type of fame that Elvis had, and that I think Michael Jackson has, the pressure of it, and the isolation that it seems to require, has gotta be really painful. I wasn't gonna let that happen to me. I wasn't gonna get to a place where I said, 'I can't go in here. I can't go to this bar. I can't go outside.' . . .

I believe that the life of a rock & roll band will last as long as you look down into the audience and can see yourself, and your audience looks up at you and can see themselves—and as long as those reflections are human, realistic ones. The biggest gift that your fans can give you is just treatin' you like a human being, because anything else dehumanizes you. And that's one of the things that has shortened the life spans, both physically and creatively, of some of the best rock & roll musicians—that cruel isolation."

publicity (including the covers of both *Time* and *Newsweek*), a legal entanglement kept him from recording for years. When he finally released an album in 1978, the somber *Darkness on the Edge of Town* received a mixed response from critics and fans.

Not until the mideighties did Springsteen find a wide audience. By this time his sometimes-wordy songwriting had become sparse and lean, his crack band was at the peak of its powers, and he released in 1984 the album many consider his masterpiece, a mixture of musical spareness and lyrical hope.

Born in the USA was the breakthrough "the Boss" had long sought; the single "Dancing in the Dark" shot to the top five and the album remained in the top ten for over two years. The nation underwent a bout of Bruce fever, responding wildly to his working-class roots and fervent patriotism (including a misguided use of Springsteen lyrics in a speech by President Reagan).

For his part, Springsteen used his newfound fame to further the liberal political causes that had long concerned him; as he once remarked, "People deserve truth, they deserve honesty . . . and the best music is there to provide you something to face the world with."[106]

Socially Committed

The passionate political and social concerns of Springsteen and U2 were shared by other rockers in the eighties. The decade saw increasing numbers of musicians taking stands and raising money for various causes.

George Harrison had pioneered the practice with his benefit concert for Bangladesh in 1971, followed by a massive 1979 concert in New York's Madison Square Garden for the antinuclear organization MUSE (Musicians United for Safe Energy).

The most prominent organizer of eighties charity events was Irish rocker Bob Geldof. Moved by the plight of famine victims in Ethiopia, he cowrote "Do They Know It's Christmas" in 1984 and arranged for its recording by a large group of celebrity musicians, raising about $13 million. A similar single recorded in 1985, "We Are the World," featured, among others, Geldof, Jackson, Springsteen, Bob Dylan, Ray Charles, Tina Turner, Diana Ross, Paul Simon, and Stevie Wonder. Although the record was artistically bland, it raised an estimated $40 million for the needy in Africa.

Geldof was the prime force behind the staging of another enormous charity event, Live Aid. It raised about $120 million in 1985 when some 1.5 billion viewers watched the broadcast of simultaneous concerts in London and Philadelphia featuring Madonna, Paul McCartney, Queen, David Bowie, U2, Judas Priest, Led Zeppelin, Duran Duran, and Phil Collins (who flew from Europe to America on the Concorde so he could perform at both concerts). Other massive benefits included country legend Willie Nelson's Farm Aid, which raised money for embattled family farmers in the American Midwest, and a series of tours headlined by Springsteen, Peter Gabriel, and Sting in support of the human-rights group Amnesty International.

Some observers have been critical of such massive charity events. They fear that funds may not reach their intended targets, and they worry that the political message may become diluted. Paul

"The Heart of Painful Events"

In this passage from The Rolling Stone History of Rock and Roll, *editor Anthony DeCurtis comments on the appeal of Bruce Springsteen's music.*

"That ability to inspire, to convey the meaning at the heart of painful events, to create a hard, uncompromising sense of purpose, is what sets Bruce Springsteen apart from his superstar peers in the rock & roll pantheon. He hasn't changed the world the way Elvis Presley or the Beatles did, and he hasn't penetrated the essence of rock & roll fervor with the fierce elegance the Stones achieved at their strongest. Dylan's astonishing run of revolutionary masterworks in the mid-Sixties sets a standard that Springsteen will never attain; he can't sing as spectacularly well as Marvin Gaye or Otis Redding, or dance with the physical genius of Michael Jackson. But if you want an artist whose work, both on record and onstage, compels a compassionate understanding of people's actual lives—their emotions and imaginings, their jobs and their play—you have nowhere to go in the realm of rock & roll but to Bruce Springsteen."

Many critics and fans saw Bruce Springsteen as the antidote for rock and roll's doldrums in the early 1980s.

Friedlander comments, "Political controversy is dangerous . . . and does not sell records like other topics such as sex and (safe) rebellion."[107]

Organizers of charity events have defended their actions by saying that their primary intention is to raise the consciousness of their audiences. "I never said we were going to stop world poverty or world hunger," remarks Bob Geldof. "[The function] was to raise the issue to the top of the political agenda, and we did that."[108]

Rock the House

Like rock and pop in general, black music in the 1980s evolved in several ways that grew increasingly separate over time. It was dominated, however, by one style.

Rap, also called hip-hop, first evolved in the Bronx in the late 1970s. A transplanted Jamaican disc jockey named Kool Herc would use turntables at mobile dance parties to mix the hottest sections of several records at once, switching back and forth and improvising rapid rhymes on top

like the "toasters" of his native Jamaica.

Other musicians expanded on the idea, experimenting with scratching—repeating small bits of music rhythmically by manually moving vinyl records back and forth. The technique created a "found" music; that is, it used elements from unexpected or odd places in new combinations. As rock historian Robert Palmer writes, "In tried-and-true rock and roll fashion, hiphop absorbed elements from the musics around it and creatively recycled elements of its own past."[109]

The first commercially recorded rap song was probably the Sugar Hill Gang's 1979 single "Rapper's Delight." The song was a surprise top-forty hit and was soon followed by singles by such artists as Kurtis Blow, Fatback, Afrika Bambataa, and Grandmaster Flash; white bands as diverse as Blondie and the Clash also adapted rap for their own purposes.

Rap flourished throughout the 1980s, increasingly embraced by middle-class listeners and white teenagers and reaching ever-widening audiences. Major breakthroughs included MTV's rap program *Yo! MTV Raps*, which was a surprise hit, and

The 1980s saw the rise of the benefit concert. Musician Bob Geldof (fourth from left) was the principal force behind 1985's Live Aid, a concert to benefit famine victims in Ethiopia.

the song "Walk This Way," a widely success-ful collaboration between rappers Run DMC and white hard-rockers Aerosmith.

As rap evolved, it became a potent tool for self-expression. Chuck D of Public Enemy often characterizes rap as "black America's CNN." By this, he means that rap is a way for a national community to share politics, styles, and language without having access to mainstream media. Mikal Gilmore adds that rap can be "a vital means of black achievement and inven-tion, [reporting on] many social realities and attitudes that most other arts and me-dia consistently ignored."[110]

Artistically, rap developed into several distinct styles. Some focused on romance, others on the hard realities of violence and urban rage. Several prominent rap-pers, including Tupac Shakur and the No-torious B.I.G., have become victims of the violent lifestyles they depicted in their mu-sic. Nonetheless, rap has become an ac-cepted and even integral part of the popular music scene, as newer artists con-tinue to expand and evolve it. Robert Palmer notes that "compared to the guitar band scene, [rap's] vitality is beyond ques-tion."[111]

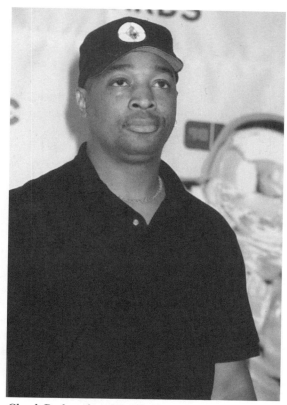

Chuck D, founder of Public Enemy, was one of the pioneers of the politically charged style of music called rap.

"Smells Like Teen Spirit"

Grunge, the style of music that has domi-nated hard rock in the nineties, can di-rectly trace its roots to the punk and postpunk movements as well as to various factions of garage rock and metal. Like every other genre in rock, in other words, grunge borrows heavily and freely from many sources. Kurt Cobain, the former leader of Nirvana, grunge's most famous

band, once wryly commented, "All in all, we sound like the Knack and the Bay City Rollers being molested by Black Flag and Black Sabbath."[112]

Grunge developed in relative obscurity in Seattle, Washington, and exploded into the national consciousness with Nirvana's surprise 1992 hit song, the deeply cynical "Smells Like Teen Spirit." Played heavily on campus radio stations, the single fo-cused massive attention on the home-grown Seattle scene.

Bands like Alice in Chains, Mudhoney, and Soundgarden became internationally famous virtually overnight. Sub Pop, a tiny label associated with many grunge bands,

Drugs and Rock and Roll

Widespread abuse of drugs and alcohol has been a major part of the rock-and-roll life from the music's beginnings, through sixties psychedelia, to more recent idioms such as punk and grunge. In his book The Map: Rediscovering Rock and Roll, *Paul Williams reflects on the drug culture.*

"Drugs and alcohol play a huge part in the history of rock and roll, as they do in the history of jazz. Today there are major figures in the rock world who are known for not being drug users or drinkers. . . . This is news, this comes almost as a surprise, and it suggests that the music may survive, that it may be possible to be a risk-taking, highly creative rock and roller exposed to the roller coaster of performing and fame and the business and all the pressures—and yet not succumb to the temptations that have killed or severely damaged so many rock stars in the past, and that are still killing 'em or rendering 'em useless today."

The career of Nirvana's Kurt Cobain (third from left) was cut short by drug addiction.

suddenly swelled into a huge business. Pearl Jam, a band that was more in the traditional hard-rock vein but came from Seattle and emerged at the same time, was lumped in with grunge and went on to become one of the biggest bands of the decade.

Nirvana had a tragically short time on top of the music scene. Cobain, always tormented by his fame and struggling (like many grunge musicians) with a heroin addiction, became increasingly erratic before committing suicide in 1994. His death shocked fans worldwide and, in the years since the tragedy, has been seen by many as the final wedge driving apart the separate factions of pop music. Some critics feel there will never again be a rock star with an appeal as universal as that of Elvis or the Beatles.

However, the story of rock is far from over; the death of rock has been predicted many times, only to have it emerge, refreshed and renewed, in new and unexpected ways. Perhaps, as Danny and the Juniors put it back in 1958, rock and roll is here to stay.

The Music Rolls On

The best rock music will always . . . give root to our past while describing our present, and thus suggest the sound of a possible future.

— critic Ken Tucker

And so it goes. Rock has evolved from its primitive, rebellious roots to include ultra-sophisticated compositions that embrace influences from all over the world. What once was dangerous, subversive outsider music is today the stuff of supermarket background sounds and television jingles. It once terrified responsible adults; now even the president of the United States digs it.

No one knows what the future of rock holds. Some say that, despite valiant efforts, it will never again achieve the raw energy and passion of the early days; the established music industry, these observers argue, has too firm a grip on what sells and what doesn't. Rock critic Timothy White laments that "rock has grown into a gigantic entertainment juggernaut in which even the most splendid displays of 'talent' and 'vision' can be of synthetic origin."[113]

Some say that rock is here for good but that the music scene has permanently fragmented. According to critic Mikal Gilmore,

There is no longer a center to popular music, no longer any one single, real mainstream. Instead, there are many diverse mainstreams. . . each representing its own perspective. . . . About the only thing today's pop world might agree on is *not* to agree on too many shared tastes or tenets [beliefs].[114]

Influences from Around the World

One thing seems certain: Rock and roll has always been, and always will be, in a permanent state of evolution and change. One style influences the next, and the one after that borrows from three or four previous styles. The result, on occasion, is something that no one has ever heard before.

Increasingly, these influences have come from around the world. Over the course of nearly half a century, rockers have had access to increasingly sophisticated methods of recording and communication; the result has been greater access to new and different styles. In the fifties a new rhythm from New Orleans, a vocal inflection from Chicago, or a guitar lick from Texas was thrilling; these days, everything from Brazilian sambas to Greek,

Arab, or African pop is readily available to inspire musicians.

Just as reggae influenced punk in the 1980s, so does this so-called world music influence rock today. Peter Gabriel, Paul Simon, David Byrne, and Robbie Robertson are just a few prominent rockers who have forged their own musical gifts with influences as diverse as Brazilian rhythms, Native American singing, and African instruments.

As rock critic Daisann Mclane writes, "Access to this astonishing diversity of music was one of the major bonuses of the nineties: it was like suddenly walking into your local supermarket and finding couscous and sushi."[115]

Blasts from the Past

Many of today's rockers, meanwhile, are content to carry on and embroider the traditions of the past.

Living legends from almost every era of rock are still at it. Even Chuck Berry and Little Richard, two of the first wave of rockers, still perform occasionally. Berry's songs are so well known the world over that he is famous for flying into a gig with only his guitar; backup bands who know his songs perfectly are always on hand.

The Rolling Stones, Paul McCartney, Stevie Wonder, Eric Clapton, Michael Jackson, Van Morrison, Joni Mitchell, James Brown, Bob Dylan, Elton John, and the Jimmy Page/Robert Plant nucleus of Led Zeppelin are only a few of the legends still doing essentially what they have always done. Until the death of Jerry Garcia in 1995, the Grateful Dead maintained a wildly devoted following. And Keith

Richards has repeatedly stated that he will keep on rocking as long as he can be wheeled onstage.

Styles of rock continue to have their standard-bearers as well. Bands like U2 and Pearl Jam continue the tradition of grandly scaled, crashing rock and roll. REM maintains the jangly folk-rock pioneered by the Byrds. Singers like Sarah McLachlan, Billy Bragg, Beck, Tracy Chapman, John Hiatt, and Jewel enlarge and extend the singer-songwriter tradition. Melissa Ethridge and John Mellencamp push forward in the working-class, eloquent storytelling tradition of Bruce Springsteen.

Blues Traveller carries on the tradition of flashy, blues-influenced rock. Oasis sustains the tradition of Beatles-like songwriting and harmony vocals (not to mention the Kinks-like tradition of sibling battles). And genres from the past such as rockabilly, heavy metal, and psychedelia continue to enjoy perodic revivals.

Some musicians remain in the limelight though they are no longer performing—or even alive. Elvis Presley albums continue to sell in massive quantities, and newly released recordings by Jimi Hendrix are eagerly awaited. Likewise, after a 1996 retrospective, the Beatles essentially topped their own seemingly untoppable act. The London *Observer* notes that "the Beatles have achieved what every group since them has failed to do: become bigger than the Beatles."[116]

Museum Quality

One benchmark of how rock has grown and changed in the years since it began is

Who Knew?

Paul Williams, in his book The Map: Rediscovering Rock and Roll, *comments on the overwhelming diversity and longevity of rock.*

"'Rock and roll is here to stay' and 'roll over, Beethoven' were heartfelt boasts, adolescent swagger, in rock's beginning years. Who would ever have imagined they might turn out to be true?. . . The phrase 'rock and roll' has never gone out of style. . . . People say, 'I love rock and roll' like it's a core part of who they are, and it is. The words 'pop music' don't begin to have anything like the same effect. Why?. . . As many deaths as it's died, overwhelmed with its own excessiveness, arrogance, pomposity, greed, becalmed as it has so often been the seas of commercial acceptance, comfort, petty power plays, the distortions and ultimately the boredom of fame, why does it always find a new vitality, how does it manage constantly to return to life, as relevant and fiery as ever?"

the world-class museum devoted to it. The music that once defined rebelliousness and throwaway pop culture is now enshrined in glass in the Rock and Roll Hall of Fame and Museum in Cleveland, Ohio. Though some rock fans shake their heads in dismay at the prospect, the museum underlines the concept that rock is, in rock historian Robert Palmer's phrase, a "living tradition."

Before Cleveland's museum opened in the fall of 1995, several pioneering rockers were inducted into the Hall of Fame. Many names have been added since, but the first ceremony in 1986 acknowledged the following trailblazers: Chuck Berry (inducted by Keith Richards); James Brown (inducted by Steve Winwood); Ray Charles (inducted by Quincy Jones); Sam Cooke (inducted by Herb Alpert); Fats Domino (inducted by Billy Joel); the Everly Brothers (inducted by Neil Young); Buddy Holly (inducted by John Fogerty); Little Richard (inducted by Roberta Flack); Jerry Lee Lewis (inducted by Hank Williams Jr.); and Elvis Presley (inducted by Sean and Julian Lennon).

Trying to predict the future of rock is a hopeless task. Will the next big thing be dance music like electronica? A variation on rap or techno-pop? An extension of thrash metal? Will it come from somewhere outside America? Or will it be something else altogether? Robert Palmer asserts, "Nobody really knows which of today's sounds will prove of lasting value—*nobody*."[117]

Of course, this uncertainty is one big reason why listening to rock is so much fun.

Notes

Introduction: The River of Rock

1. Bill Flanagan, *Written in My Soul.* Chicago: Contemporary Books, 1986, p. 5.

2. Robert Palmer, *Rock and Roll: An Unruly History.* New York: Harmony Books, 1995, p. 76.

Chapter 1: Growing from the Roots

3. Flanagan, *Written in My Soul,* p. 9.

4. Quoted in Timothy White, *Rock Lives.* New York: Henry Holt, 1990, p. 720.

5. Quoted in Anthony DeCurtis and James Heinke, eds., *The Rolling Stone History of Rock and Roll.* New York: Random House/Rolling Stone Press, 1992, p. 3.

6. Palmer, *Rock and Roll,* pp. 210–11.

7. Paul Friedlander, *Rock and Roll: A Social History.* New York: Westview/HarperCollins, 1996, p. 19.

Chapter 2: The First Rock Explosion

8. Quoted in Palmer, *Rock and Roll,* p. 202.

9. Quoted in Palmer, *Rock and Roll,* p. 8.

10. Quoted in White, *Rock Lives,* p. 77.

11. Quoted in *Rolling Stone* eds., *The Rolling Stone Interviews 1967–80.* New York: Rolling Stone Press, 1981, p. 224.

12. Quoted in DeCurtis and Heinke, *The Rolling Stone History of Rock and Roll,* p. 60.

13. Quoted in DeCurtis and Heinke, *The Rolling Stone History of Rock and Roll,* p. 51.

14. Quoted in DeCurtis and Heinke, *The Rolling Stone History of Rock and Roll,* p. 54.

15. Quoted in Ed Ward, Geoffrey Stokes, and Ken Tucker, *Rock of Ages: The Rolling Stone History of Rock and Roll.* New York: Rolling Stone Press, 1986, p. 149.

16. Quoted in Friedlander, *Rock and Roll,* p. 23.

17. Friedlander, *Rock and Roll,* p. 21.

18. Quoted in Jonathan Eisen, ed., *The Age of Rock 2.* New York: Random House, 1970, p. 338.

Chapter 3: Pop Moves In: The Music Industry Discovers Rock and Roll

19. Quoted in David P. Szatmary, *Rockin' in Time.* Englewood Cliffs, NJ: Prentice-Hall, 1987, p. 52.

20. John Tobler, *Thirty Years of Rock.* New York: Exeter Books, 1985, p. 36.

21. Ward, Stokes, and Tucker, *Rock of Ages,* p. 245.

22. Quoted in Szatmary, *Rockin' in Time,* p. 53.

23. Charlie Gillett, *The Sound of the City.* New York: Pantheon Books, 1983, p. 43.

24. Quoted in DeCurtis and Heinke, *The Rolling Stone History of Rock and Roll,* p. 108.

25. Author interview with Sonny Bono in Palm Springs, California, 1988.

26. Quoted in Ward, Stokes, and Tucker, *Rock of Ages,* p. 327.

27. Quoted in Friedlander, *Rock and Roll,* p. 71.

28. Tobler, *Thirty Years of Rock,* p. 49.

29. Palmer, *Rock and Roll,* p. 137.

Chapter 4: The British Invasion

30. Quoted in Clinton Heylin, ed., *The Penguin Book of Rock and Roll Writing.* New York: Viking Penguin, 1992, p. 160.

31. Quoted in Hunter Davies, *The Beatles.* New York: McGraw-Hill, 1978, p. 30.

32. Quoted in Gareth L. Pawlowki, *How They Became the Beatles.* New York: Dutton, 1989, p. 156.

33. Quoted in George Martin, *All You Need Is Ears.* New York: St. Martin's Press, 1979, p. 159.

34. Quoted in Philip Norman, *Shout!* New York: Simon and Schuster, 1981, p. 224.

35. Szatmary, *Rockin' in Time*, p. 82.

36. Quoted in DeCurtis and Heinke, *The Rolling Stone History of Rock and Roll*, p. 199.

37. Tobler, *Thirty Years of Rock*, p. 78.

38. Quoted in Palmer, *Rock and Roll: An Unruly History*, p. 113.

39. Quoted in Flanagan, *Written in My Soul*, p. 375.

40. Ward, Stokes, and Tucker, *Rock of Ages*, p. 285.

41. Quoted in Kurt Loder, *Bat Chain Puller.* New York: St. Martin's Press, 1990, p. 145.

42. Quoted in Szatmary, *Rockin' in Time*, p. 83.

43. Quoted in Friedlander, *Rock and Roll*, p. 125.

44. Ward, Stokes, and Tucker, *Rock of Ages*, p. 359.

45. Quoted in *Rolling Stone* eds., *The Rolling Stone Interviews 1967–80*, p. 241.

46. Quoted in *Rolling Stone* eds., *The Rolling Stone Interviews 1967–80*, p. 35.

Chapter 5: That Sweet Soul Music

47. Quoted in DeCurtis and Heinke, *The Rolling Stone History of Rock and Roll*, pp. 260–61.

48. Quoted in Palmer, *Rock and Roll*, p. 243.

49. Quoted in Scott Cohen, *Yakety Yak.* New York: Fireside, 1994, p. 158.

50. Quoted in DeCurtis and Heinke, *The Rolling Stone History of Rock and Roll*, pp. 275–76.

51. Friedlander, *Rock and Roll*, p. 12.

52. Ward, Stokes, and Tucker, *Rock of Ages*, p. 235.

53. Quoted in *Rolling Stone* eds., *The Rolling Stone Interviews 1967–80*, p. 71.

54. Quoted in Ward, Stokes, and Tucker, *Rock of Ages*, p. 297.

55. Quoted in Palmer, *Rock and Roll*, p. 86.

56. Quoted in Patricia Romanowski and Holly George-Warren, eds., *The New Rolling Stone Encyclopedia of Rock and Roll.* New York: Rolling Stone Press, 1995, p. 839.

57. Ward, Stokes, and Tucker, *Rock of Ages*, p. 273.

58. Quoted in DeCurtis and Heinke, *The Rolling Stone History of Rock and Roll*, p. 334.

59. Quoted in Jonathan Buckley and Mark Ellingham, eds., *Rock: The Rough Guide*, London: Rough Guide Press, 1996, p. 334.

Chapter 6: The Sixties: Rock Explodes

60. Quoted in Philip Norman, *Shout!*, pp. 292–93.

61. Ward, Stokes, and Tucker, *Rock of Ages*, p. 329.

62. Quoted in White, *Rock Lives*, p. 269.

63. Quoted in DeCurtis and Heinke, *The Rolling Stone History of Rock and Roll*, p. 372.

64. Quoted in Friedlander, *Rock and Roll*, p. 224.

65. Quoted in DeCurtis and Heinke, *The Rolling Stone History of Rock and Roll*, p. 418.

66. Quoted in Palmer, *Rock and Roll*, p. 102.

67. Quoted in *Rolling Stone* eds., *The Rolling Stone Interviews 1967–80*, p. 15.

68. Mikal Gilmore, *Night Beat.* New York: Doubleday, 1998, p. 56.

69. Ward, Stokes, and Tucker, *Rock of Ages*, p. 377.

70. Quoted in Ward, Stokes, and Tucker, *Rock of Ages*, p. 431.

71. Ward, Stokes, and Tucker, *Rock of Ages*, p. 409.

Chapter 7: The Early Seventies

72. Quoted in Loder, *Bat Chain Puller*, p. 152.

73. Quoted in *Rolling Stone* eds., *The Rolling Stone Interviews 1967–80*, p. 290.

74. Patrick MacDonald, "Morrison and Mitchell: As Good as It Gets," *Seattle Times*, May 14, 1998, p. 95.

75. Quoted in Bruce Pollock, *In Their Own Words*. New York: Macmillan, 1975, p. 169.

76. Quoted in Cohen, *Yakety Yak*, p. 158.

77. White, *Rock Lives*, p. 288.

78. White, *Rock Lives*, p. 430.

79. Gilmore, *Night Beat*, p. 242.

80. Palmer, *Rock and Roll*, p. 249.

81. Quoted in Ward, Stokes, and Tucker, *Rock of Ages*, p. 533.

82. Quoted in DeCurtis and Heinke, *The Rolling Stone History of Rock and Roll*, p. 523.

Chapter 8: New Energy from the Underground

83. Quoted in Ward, Stokes, and Tucker, *Rock of Ages*, p. 522.

84. Quoted in Scott Schinder, ed., *Rolling Stone's Alt-Rock-A-Rama*. New York: Delta/Dell, 1996, p. 9.

85. Quoted in DeCurtis and Heinke, *The Rolling Stone History of Rock and Roll*, p. 348.

86. Quoted in Palmer, *Rock and Roll*, p. 270.

87. Loder, *Bat Chain Puller*, p. 367.

88. Quoted in Heylin, *The Penguin Book of Rock and Roll Writing*, p. 197.

89. Tobler, *Thirty Years of Rock*, p. 195.

90. Quoted in Buckley and Ellingham, *Rock*, p. 769.

91. Quoted in Ward, Stokes, and Tucker, *Rock of Ages*, p. 555.

92. Quoted in Flanagan, *Written in My Soul*, p. 198.

93. Loder, *Bat Chain Puller*, p. 345.

94. Quoted in Schinder, *Rolling Stone's Alt-Rock-A-Rama*, p. 299.

95. Quoted in Palmer, *Rock and Roll*, p. 278.

96. Gilmore, *Night Beat*, p. 165.

97. Quoted in Ward, Stokes, and Tucker, *Rock of Ages*, p. 508.

Chapter 9: The Eighties and Nineties

98. Quoted in DeCurtis and Heinke, *The Rolling Stone History of Rock and Roll*, pp. 685–86.

99. Loder, *Bat Chain Puller*, p. 260.

100. Quoted in Romanowski and George-Warren, *The New Rolling Stone Encyclopedia of Rock and Roll*, p. x.

101. Quoted in DeCurtis and Heinke, *The Rolling Stone History of Rock and Roll*, p. 653.

102. Friedlander, *Rock and Roll*, p. 269.

103. Quoted in DeCurtis and Heinke, *The Rolling Stone History of Rock and Roll*, p. 662.

104. Quoted in DeCurtis and Heinke, *The Rolling Stone History of Rock and Roll*, p. 609.

105. Quoted in DeCurtis and Heinke, *The Rolling Stone History of Rock and Roll*, p. 620.

106. Quoted in Buckley and Ellingham, *Rock*, p. 831.

107. Friedlander, *Rock and Roll*, p. 267.

108. Quoted in Romanowski and George-Warren, *The New Rolling Stone Encyclopedia of Rock and Roll*, p. 107.

109. Palmer, *Rock and Roll*, p. 282.

110. Gilmore, *Night Beat*, p. 390.

111. Palmer, *Rock and Roll*, p. 290.

112. Quoted in Buckley and Ellingham, *Rock*, p. 610.

Epilogue: The Music Rolls On

113. White, *Rock Lives*, p. 510.

114. Gilmore, *Night Beat*, pp. 39–40.

115. Quoted in DeCurtis and Heinke, *The Rolling Stone History of Rock and Roll*, p. 663.

116. Quoted in Gilmore, *Night Beat*, p. 39.

117. Palmer, *Rock and Roll*, p. 289.

For Further Reading

Scott Cohen, *Yakety Yak*. New York: Fireside, 1994. A collection of "interviews" (the answers to some very oddball questions), this book is like much of pop music: dumb and junky, but a lot of fun.

Pete Fornatale, *The Story of Rock 'n' Roll*. New York: William Morrow, 1987. Written by a veteran rock radio personality, this compact and clearly written history includes a foreword by Graham Nash.

Stuart A. Kallen, *History of Rock and Roll*. Bloomington, MN: Abdo and Daughters, 1989. An extremely basic, multivolume decade-by-decade history.

James Kerr, ed., *Rock World*. New York: Crestwood House, 1992. A simple multivolume series focusing on particular subjects: concerts, videos, and stars.

Ron Knapp, *American Legends of Rock*. Springfield, NJ: Enslow, 1996. This book is a series of brief but informative profiles of a handful of important rockers, from Chuck Berry to Bruce Springsteen.

Patricia Romanowski and Holly George-Warren, eds., *The New Rolling Stone Encyclopedia of Rock and Roll*. New York: Rolling Stone Press, 1995. An exhaustive alphabetic listing. The most accurate, evenhanded, informative, and easy-to-use of the many rock encyclopedias available.

David Shirley, *The History of Rock and Roll*. New York: Franklin Watts, 1997. A well-written overview of the music, though hampered by a lack of information on the early roots of the blues, gospel, and country.

John Tobler, *Thirty Years of Rock*. New York: Exeter Books, 1985. A large-format, glossy book by a veteran British music writer, this is a quick overview without reference to historical context, but it has some worthwhile photos.

Works Consulted

Jonathan Buckley and Mark Ellingham, eds., *Rock: The Rough Guide*. London: Rough Guide Press, 1996. A guide developed by British editors who solicited highly opinionated contributions on the Internet. Although too much space is given to obscure groups, it is fascinating nonetheless.

Hunter Davies, *The Beatles*. New York: McGraw-Hill, 1978. A revised edition of the authorized biography. Heavily censored but basically factual. Originally written in 1968, with a short chapter added to bring its history up to 1978.

Anthony DeCurtis and James Heinke, eds., *The Rolling Stone History of Rock and Roll*. New York: Random House/Rolling Stone Press, 1992. Probably the single best source of information and photos on rock, this is the latest revised edition of a book first published in 1980. Its concise, thoughtful, and sometimes highly personal essays were written by some of music's best critics and scholars.

Jonathan Eisen, ed., *The Age of Rock 2*. New York: Random House, 1970. This collection of articles and writings, by a variety of journalists and musicians, dates primarily from the late 1960s.

Bill Flanagan, *Written in My Soul*. Chicago: Contemporary Books, 1986. A series of interviews by the executive editor of *Musician* magazine with rock songwriters about their craft.

Paul Friedlander, *Rock and Roll: A Social History*. New York: Westview/Harper-Collins, 1996. This concise and rather dry history by a musician and professor of popular music is designed for use as a college textbook, placing the music analytically in the context of social change.

Charlie Gillett, *The Sound of the City*. New York: Pantheon Books, 1983. A revised and updated version of a 1970 book by a British writer and disc jockey. One of the first histories of the origins and early days of rock, this is rather dry but still a classic.

Mikal Gilmore, *Night Beat*. New York: Doubleday, 1998. A book of incisive and highly readable essays, reviews, and interviews by a veteran writer for *Rolling Stone* and other publications.

Clinton Heylin, ed., *The Penguin Book of Rock and Roll Writing*. New York: Viking Penguin, 1992. A collection of writings about the music, from the beginnings to the present, by critics, musicians, and others. Sometimes outrageous, sometimes trivial, sometimes important, rarely dull.

Kurt Loder, *Bat Chain Puller*. New York: St. Martin's Press, 1990. An excellent collection of essays and interviews by a longtime rock critic, this book focuses on the ways rock music and celebrity interact.

George Martin, *All You Need Is Ears*. New York: St. Martin's Press, 1979. A memoir by the Beatles' longtime producer.

Patrick MacDonald, "Morrison and Mitchell: As Good as It Gets," *Seattle Times*, May 14, 1998. Newspaper rock critic reviews a live show and changing music styles of Van Morrison and Joni Mitchell.

Legs McNeil and Gillian McCain, *Please Kill Me: The Uncensored History of Punk.* New York: Grove Press, 1996. An oral history detailing the rise and fall of punk, this book was cowritten by Legs McNeil, who claims to have coined the term *punk.*

Philip Norman, *Shout!* New York: Simon and Schuster, 1981. Easily the most thorough, fully researched and fair-minded of all the books on the Beatles.

Robert Palmer, *Rock and Roll: An Unruly History.* New York: Harmony Books, 1995. Not a straightforward history, but essential reading for anyone interested in the subject, this book was written by one of America's most distinguished writers on popular music. It accompanies the fascinating ten-hour PBS series *Rock and Roll,* which itself is an excellent and intelligent introduction to the music, with scores of wonderful interviews and performance clips.

Gareth L. Pawlowski, *How They Became the Beatles.* New York: Dutton, 1989. An obsessively detailed history of the Beatles' early years. Worth looking at for the wonderful early memorabilia, including newspaper clippings, photos, and posters.

Bruce Pollock, *In Their Own Words.* New York: Macmillan, 1975. An interesting collection of interviews with pop songwriters, from the Brill Building era forward, on the ins and outs of their craft.

Rolling Stone eds., *The Rolling Stone Interviews 1967–80.* New York: Rolling Stone Press, 1981. A fascinating collection of in-depth, firsthand interviews with many of the seminal musicians in rock.

Scott Schinder, ed., *Rolling Stone's Alt-Rock-A-Rama.* New York: Delta/Dell, 1996. A funny and irreverent look at many aspects of the alternative music scene, which is broadly defined here to include many aspects of modern rock. Many of the contributions are by musicians.

David P. Szatmary, *Rockin' in Time.* Englewood Cliffs, NJ: Prentice-Hall, 1987. Designed as a textbook, this volume is out of date but has some interesting details.

Ed Ward, Geoffrey Stokes, and Ken Tucker, *Rock of Ages: The Rolling Stone History of Rock and Roll.* New York: Rolling Stone Press, 1986. This extremely detailed study is an excellent adjunct to the Illustrated History series of essays also published by *Rolling Stone* magazine. It is in need of an update for the past decade; until then, *Rolling Stone's Alt-Rock-A-Rama* and other more recent volumes will have to do.

Timothy White, *Rock Lives.* New York: Henry Holt, 1990. A massive volume of profiles and interviews by a veteran rock historian, this is full of fascinating information but is also sometimes windy and pretentious.

Paul Williams, *The Map: Rediscovering Rock and Roll.* South Bend, IN: And Books, 1988. This philosophical book, written by the founder of *Crawdaddy,* the first magazine of rock criticism, is self-indulgent but thought-provoking.

Index

Picture Credits

About the Author

An enthusiastic music fan since childhood, Adam Woog is the author of many books for young adults, including volumes for Lucent Books on Louis Armstrong, Duke Ellington, Elvis Presley, and the Beatles. He lives in his home town, Seattle, Washington, with his wife and daughter.